THE FUTURE WILL NOT INVOLVE UNDERWEAR

PATRICK MCNERTHNEY

Illustrated by
MICHI MATHIAS ILLUSTRATION & COMICS

CONTENTS

SHORTS

LONGER

For Paige

SHORTS

SLEDGE HAMMER! WOULD DO IT

I magine my surprise when the car started to slide down the mountain just a bit.

The antilock brakes were doing that horrible rumble/bump thing, which is typically the first clue that something's amiss, coupled with the fact that I didn't want to go downhill anymore, yet we were still going downhill more.

My son asked what was up. I forgot he was there. I calmly replied that the antilock brakes were acting up, likely because the car is leased, which is why you should never lease a vehicle. I always lie to my son but still want to give him practical life advice whenever possible.

Eventually I realized what had to be done, which was to toboggan toward the rocky side of the snow-and-ice-covered road and run into the nearest convenient rock. It worked. Despite thousands of years of technological evolution, icy rocks are still the best way to stop moving vehicles. And take out frustration on laptops.

Nature can get really cold, it turns out. On this day it was an unseasonable 22 degrees. We wouldn't die, but I really didn't want to walk eight miles down the mountain to flag down someone on the highway. Nor did I want to go ask for help from the guy I saw shoveling hay with a pitchfork earlier, because although he was nice when I said "good morning," I sensed he lived on a mountain so he didn't have to deal with people.

I thought perhaps this was punishment for wanting to shoot grouse. That's what we were there for. We just shoot them and leave them as a warning to other grouse not to mess with us. Okay fine, we eat them — "harvest the land," as it were — but not this time, for the Great Grouse Gods were displeased with our presence, as was the mountain.

Eventually I was able to reverse back from the rock, then kind of slide down the rest of the road at four miles an hour while telling myself and my son over and over, "Trust me, I know what I'm doing." That's my favorite quote from the '80s show *Sledge Hammer!* It's worth a look.

The point of the story is to always take crazy risks with your kid in the car to show said kid that life is about managing critical situations while looking cool. I'm sure he thought I looked cool, with my sweaty brow and white-knuckle grip on the wheel. But in my mind, I looked like Brad Pitt in *Ocean's Eleven*. Or something like that.

"BITTER LIKE A SNAKE" IS A PHRASE

My son has a snake; it's orange and white with red beady eyes of death.

Its name is Creamsicle. A highly coveted, newsworthy snake, not new to the press. You may have seen it on the *Today Show*.*

*I find this show terrifying.

I'm sure when my son moves out of the house, we'll end up adopting this thing.

It has no emotions. C'mon, it's a snake. Well, I guess it has basic ones like fear, based on the instinct to stay alive. And perhaps bitterness, when it sees us playing with the dog.

But that's the problem: By its very nature it wants to eat my dog. Biologically speaking, that is. Just like a banker wants to lend you more money than you can afford to pay back. Neither snake nor banker has outright admitted any of this to me, but certainly the distinct absence of a moral compass is the common thread weaving through these two sentient beings, thus firmly ensconcing them on the path to a searing, burning hell.

Creamsicle is currently on Day 24 of an official hunger strike. That's what the pet store people call it when snakes don't eat.

I call this union-like strike a waste of my time and money. It works like this: Every Tuesday, I drive to the store-where-we-buy-live-rodents, purchase the alive-disgusting vermin, drive home, drop the wiggly squeaking fuzzy thing into the snake's domicile, wait till the next morning, inevitably hear my son say, "Dad, the mouse is still here," then I'm forced to dispose of the creature as humanely as possible.

My version of "humane" is "quick and ceremonial," so I set up this little guillotine made of popsicle sticks, razor blades, and tooth floss. I dress the mouse up like Louis XVI and…

I'd better stop; I don't want to sound like a weirdo.

The point of all this is to help guide you on future pet purchases. Here's my experience:

Birds — swear at you

Snakes — would kill you if they could

Mice — deserve swift, speedy deaths if left uneaten

Dogs — are lovable idiots with mildly inappropriate behavior

Cats — untrustworthy

Frogs — want to live in your mouth

Bugs — don't be friends with anyone who keeps bugs as pets

Fish — if live past one week, end up being quite entrancing

That's it. There are no other pets to choose from in the universe. Choose wisely. And try not to make your snake bitter. It makes them really aggressive.

SECRET BEDTIME HOUSE LUST

FALL 2020

I love my family.

In quarantine I frequently find myself desperately wanting to get away from them.

Wait, is what we're doing still called quarantine?

Currently I've escaped to our basement. There's a man from Orkin (pest control) down here, and it's small and cramped, and he's just standing there not doing anything, which is really awkward because he has an uncomfortable mustache (well, it's likely silky and smooth and very comfortable to him, but it makes me feel weird) and deep blue eyes, and I'm pretty sure he should be wiggling through our crawlspace checking for varmints instead of just standing there eating Cheetos (but expertly keeping the phosphorescent orange cheez powder off his silky white moustache as all facial hair aficionados are apt to do).

Maybe it's his lunch break. I wonder if he washes his hands a lot, or maybe pest control experts are apathetic toward the fact that they're covered in disease and industrial poisons between 8:00 a.m. and 5:00 p.m., so they just munch away regardless.

Still, I'd rather be down here with him than upstairs with those people.

My wife says if we just had a bigger house it wouldn't be a problem. I wholeheartedly disagree. The Notorious B.I.G.'s song "Mo Money Mo Problems" was originally titled "Mo House Mo Strife," but Sean "Diddy" Combs made a last-second edit prior to release. You can look it up.

No, a big house would be worse because they'd (wife, kid) still interrupt me to ask super annoying questions like "Honey, can we go over our spending this month so we don't dip into our savings account?" or "Dad, I like this girl but she doesn't seem to like me; what should I do?" Who do they think I am, a Suze Orman/Phil Donahue hybrid? Regardless of the fact that I'm unemployed, I don't have time to make financial decisions or become a spirit guide for some preteen's hormone-fueled inconsequential nonsense.

Plus, bigger houses just have bigger rats. You get used to rats in a small house. They become both a defining characteristic and a pleasant reminder of how awful it was to live in the 1300s and thus a warning not to experiment with time travel. Added bonus: You don't have to host for the holidays. Nothing lets you off the hook like reminding interested parties they're welcome to come by and hang out, but please refrain from using the toilet if you hear any splashing sounds. Or squeaks.

Anyway, despite my well-documented evidence to the contrary, I keep catching my wife looking at property listings in bed. IN BED. It's scandalous. At first I thought she was just eyeing her favorite Peloton instructor, Denis Morton. Denis is quite the catch — single, handsome, super funny, REALLY smart, brimming with all these bizarrely inspirational phrases I've literally turned into T-shirts. (I sent him one, although after several hours of searching for his apartment and phone number, the best I could do was locate Peloton Headquarters' address in New York, so I doubt he'll get it, thanks to the thieving tendencies of interns manning the mailrooms, more's the pity.) He's also a former Division One football player…did I mention how chiseled, perfectly sweaty, and smart he is? I mean, this morning I wrote down today's quote for future shirt or possibly poster creation: "There is no progress without failure. Just learn and go." (Sigh.) Dreamboat.

Am I still talking about Denis-with-one-*n*? Did I mention he grows his hair out, then cuts it and donates it to the charity "Wigs for Kids"? No wonder I'm still talking about him. Do you think he talks about me?

Ah, anyway, no, she's not lusting after Denis; she's looking at friggin' houses. Devastating.

The saving grace is my previously mentioned complete lack of W-2 employment. It turns out banks, with all their homespun neighborhood friendship and community support—themed advertising, only loan money if you can actually pay it back in such a way that they'll also profit from the repayment. The gall of those cigar-chomping fat cats makes my blood boil, but in this particular instance their greed and inhumanity play strongly in my favor. I don't even know what a W-2 is, but I'm glad I don't have one, because it's a one-way ticket to two-car garages, central air, at least two bathrooms (twice the rats!), and fancy screen doors all over the place.

No thanks. Plus, I heard neighborhoods with large houses are super weird, what with their block parties (a.k.a. pyramid schemes), invites to summer barbecues, sidewalk chalk—covered driveways, willingness to share lawn care equipment, community watches, etc. Again, no thanks. I've seen the freak show that happens in these places — I mean, nobody just made up *Stepford Wives*, *Your Friends and Neighbors*, and to a lesser degree *The Sopranos*. And of course, *Alien*.

So we'll stay where we are, please and thank you. It's not that bad. The rat, er, Orkin guy just left, so I'll get along just fine. Besides, the squeaks in our crawlspace are fairly easy to ignore once you get used to them.

THIRD-PARTY CANDIDATES

WINTER 2020

My holidays are filled with Holiday Towels.

Hand towels. Beach towels. Bath towels. Fuzzy towels. Threadbare towels. All shapes and sizes, towels, towels, towels. A bunch of Holiday Towels.

Towels hanging off the kitchen faucet. Towels hanging off the oven door handle. Towels hanging off this towel rack in the bathroom. Towels in the laundry basket upstairs. Towels in the laundry basket downstairs. Towels in the washing machine. Towels in the dryer. Towels on the towel storage rack. Towels on hooks. Towels in storage bins. Towels on the shelf downstairs.

If you need a Holiday Towel, let me know.

PATRICK MCNERTHNEY

We even have Halloween Towels.

Skeleton towels (white on black). Jack-o'-lantern towels (orange on black). Ghost towels (white on black again).

Thanksgiving gets skipped. What a decorating rip-off Thanksgiving is. I don't think there's even such a thing as Thanksgiving Towels.

Then of course along comes the most towel-friendly time of year: Christmas/Hanukkah/Kwanzaa/Boxing Day. Of which my household celebrates Christmas, i.e., Capitol One's Favorite Time of Year.

Snowman towels (white on green). Red Santa towels (basically red on white). Christmas tree towels (green on red).

So on and so forth.

All these Holiday Towels are very festive. You should try decorating with towels, especially if you have kids, because decorating makes you look like an involved parent concerned with their well-being and stuff — or even if you don't have kids, because it makes it look like you're a generally good-humored, celebratory person with no problems and a complete handle on life, because who else but someone with Total Confidence and Control has the time to put up a bunch of themed towels?

Either way, once you've plastered your home with these towels, make sure you take the opportunity to look in the mirror and say,

"Wow, this place looks great, and damn don't you look good today!" while giving yourself that famous knowing smile and even an encouraging wink if you're feeling coy. Because that's what the holidays are all about.

There is one slight problem with Holiday Towels. You can't actually use them to dry anything.

I know it sounds counterintuitive. Like having a formal dining set, fake plants, or a third-party candidate. But it's true.

In fact, if you even think about reaching for one of your Holiday Towels to dry your hands/a dish/the dog, the Holiday Towel Police You Live With will appear as if from nowhere to present you with a Cease & Desist, usually in the form of angry yelling.

Furthermore, you can't leave out regular, non-themed towels next to your Holiday Towels to solve the issue of daily wetness because apparently this just ruins everything on a visual level while diminishing the thousands of hours of hard work behind obtaining / storing / putting out the Holiday Towels in the first place. How dare you.

So you're just going to have to figure out a different way to dry things. Our cavepeople ancestors somehow did it; so can you. Maybe try fire.

Just remember: It's all worth it for the sake of the holidays. They'll be gone before you know it, so celebrate down to the finest detail, take the time to revel in the beauty of your now fabric-rich surroundings, and perhaps think about buying me something. Just not a towel.

EARLY ADOPTERS

FALL 2020

F all haseth arrived, and as with every year it comes with a cornucopia (or "horn of plenty," which I find much too sensual a moniker) of fresh, vibrant, and apparently controversial ideas.

For example, my wife says the neighbor is going to be upset by the gigantic inflatable turkey dinner I'm putting in our front yard once Halloween is over. There's this unfortunate gap between Halloween decorations and Christmas, er, Holiday decorations in my neighborhood. Housewives go balls-out for Halloween with the lights and the inflatables and the skeletons and even the animatronics. Then, tragically, it's all disassembled and re-stored during the dreariest of months when we need it most:

November. Alas, we're left with super ugly stoops filled with whiskey-swigging grandparents hollering at kids and threatening the mailman. Er, mailperson.

That's right, I'm going to spice up November by blowing up a 12-foot-high, properly cooked and thus salmonella-free stuffed and dressed turkey. No inflatable turduckin' here, no thank you — we're traditionalists when it comes to Thanksgiving.

Yes, depressing November, I cast thee away! My 100% nonrecyclable single-use plastic inflatable will inspire artists to come up with songs about November that don't make me want to develop a Quaalude habit. Think about all those stupid, redundant November songs: "November Rain," by Guns N' Roses (I was in the band; I played the seldom-used wind chimes, but I still got a heroin addiction), "When November Has Come," by Gorillaz, "November is My Month to Rock," by Bob Dylan, and Jimi Hendrix's famous vocal-free redo of our beloved "Star-Spangled Banner," "Trippin' on Thanksgivin' Fixin's." Well, you don't have to bear this noise any longer!

My inflatable turkey dinner set-up will inspire rap-metal fusion artists from Limp Bizkit to Kid Rock to create brand new hot tracks, including "Hold My Hand and Tell Me About Your Day and How You Feel, I'll Just Sit Here and Listen," and "No Stuffing, Dear, I Too Am

Concerned About My Elevated Blood Pressure," while enlightening the neighborhood and bringing hope and possibly cash to my doorstep.

Oh, and hope for the neighborhood/mankind/etc. too.

You should buy one and do this with me. It fills the empty 1,395 square feet of your front lawn quite nicely, prevents your neighbors from glancing through your living room window and seeing you in your underwear, and provides the perfect segue to Christmas, er, Holiday décor.

The pump that keeps it inflated with carbon monoxide runs on diesel, so it's very affordable and fits easily in your driveway or parking space — as long as you don't need to walk in that area or own a car.

To be honest, even though this anatomically correct inflatable is a great idea, it's a tough sell if you have a spouse, as I'm finding out. Especially one with a general concern for the environment or how you're perceived as citizens. My suggestion is to do what, in one way or another, all the artists we admire do when confronted by authority figures, naysayers, or doubters: Say you won't do it so you avoid the unpleasant conversation, then just do it anyway.

Don't overthink it, just do it. You'll thank me later. I'll send you a picture of mine when it's up next weekend. If you look at it every

day as inspiration, it'll help you cross the
threshold from banal "Neighbor What's-Their-
Name" to "Linda the Early Adopter." Or "There's
Frank." Or whatever your name is.

HOW TO SPOT A FUTURE PONZI SCHEMER

SUMMER 2020

Our neighborhood had an Art Walk last Saturday. It was sunny.

Normally I'm too busy (disinterested in anything of higher culture or requiring effort) to participate in "Art Walks." Hmph. Art Walks. So stupid. Who do these people think they are, Dr. Seuss? The presumptive pageantry reeks of guilty bourgeoisie compensating for their teeming wealth by slathering patchouli oil over their naked, sweaty flesh as they consume champagne and caviar atop their parapets, even though I don't actually understand Marxism.

But this year is obviously different. For normal people, at least.

So yes, I plugged my nose and prepared to bring a healthy dose of disgust to the general area located around my house.

My wife, son, and dog came along! His name is Benji. The dog. Yesterday we thought he ate a grape. It turned out to be a $277.00 ghost grape. Because somehow I've gone through 46 years of life and several dog ownership periods without knowing grapes are deathly toxic and/or poisonous to dogs.

I gave my son grapes for lunch. Well, plus some other stuff. And then a few moments later, to what apparently should have been my horror, I saw the stupid dog trying to bury something in the rug, the act of which is symbolized by an adorable albeit makes-him-look-like-an-idiot technique of sort of nosing over the item to be disappeared/buried.

You know, like a pig rooting around with its nose in the mud, kind of flipping over gross things to eat.

Then, to what definitely became my horror, my son discovered it was an errant grape that must have landed on our grape-colored (no joke) kitchen floor. Then he explained grapes can kill dogs. Which led to the *$277.00 Great Grape Panic of Monday, August 3rd, 2020*, wherein I researched via my favorite search engine, WebCrawler, and discovered a bunch of alarmist propaganda confirming that the stupid grape (not the one Benji "buried," the mystery one he may have eaten but we didn't know for sure) could easily cause liver failure and death or something.

I tried to blow it off, but the kid was crying because he actually cares about living things (gets it from his mother), so I called the vet, who confirmed Benji the Dog Wonder should be brought in for a fun stomach pump.

No grape was found. Benji is alive. It's for the best. Cost: $277.00.

So the family and the dog and I are walking around on Saturday at the Because of COVID Art Fair, and even though I had my practiced sneer ready to rock, it turned out to be quite the impressive occasion. All of these moderately attractive to attractive people displayed their wares (for capitalist retail sale, but I chose to overlook this vulgar display of oozing greed for the sake of my family) in kind of cool ways, many utilizing their fences as marketing communication tools or art holders or in some select cases as ways to keep me out of their homes.

Better yet, several up-and-coming Wall Street Trader/Ponzi Scheme Developers aged four to eight showed quite a bit of initiative by proffering various food and beverage items for sale at absurdly low prices, likely a benefit

of not having to establish a true Cost of Goods metric or line item for Overhead in their Profit and Loss statements since this Limited Liability Company or possibly S Corp was wittingly and/or unwittingly funded by the homeowner/parent(s) who will likely claim it as a charitable deduction on their 2020 taxes.

Thus I got a good deal on some chocolate chip cookies and lemonade.

Someone else sold macaroons out of her cute Volkswagen van, but she seemed to be a legit businessperson. Shame on her.

The moral of the story: Don't trust artists because they're all greedy, money-grubbing richies, but it's kind of nice to experience their bizarre rituals if you're ever super bored anytime soon. Plus it's summer. You should get outside.

BEWARE THE END CAP

The great 2020 Halloween debate in our neighborhood revolved around how to dispense candy. We were officially the only neighborhood in the country struggling to come to terms with this dilemma. We did the research. It's true.

Several houses chose the Pipe Delivery Method. Since you may not intellectually understand the principles behind this method, we will herein describe it to you in grave detail. Yeah…ah? Grave detail? Come on, I'm swinging for the fences here; they can't all be home runs.

It works like this: A cylinder of some form, likely constructed of heavily refined petroleum products (which you may not know come from dinosaurs), is purchased at, and only at, Home

Depot, or possibly stolen from a construction site.

It's then shoved into a small-to-mid-sized sedan, with most of the pipe protruding from the sunroof, and driven home while you try to avoid eye contact with other motorists who think you're a loser for driving a small-to-mid-sized sedan because it's just so lame and it exacerbates the easily winded, middle-aged father vibe you have going on.

Upon your glorious arrival home, where your family undoubtedly has gathered on the front porch to cheer and embrace you as they always do when you leave for a bit, a series of spikes or other deterrents are added to the delivery device, in an effort to discourage greedy little four-year-olds from getting their grubby paws all over it in their frenzy to gorge themselves on the thrice-refined corn syrup-laden miniature candy bars you fell victim to purchasing because the End Cap/Point-of-Purchase displays are just so effective on you and it's hopeless to resist. Which is why you frequently find your house stocked with far too many batteries, eyeglass repair kits, lip balms, and *People* magazines.

Interesting fact: Thrice-refined corn syrup actually comes from cows.

(Also, according to additional research, electricity was this year's most popular little kid deterrent. We do lots of research.)

After your tube is appropriately booby-trapped, in comes the moment of truth. Do you have enough slope to utilize the mysterious force physics professors at major universities still struggle to understand, let alone agree on what to name, to transform the potential energy found in a patiently waiting Snickers bar into the kinetic death energy of movement, thus propelling it to the designated candy retrieval zone you marked with a huge chalk *X* like in a Road Runner cartoon and furthermore covered in shards of broken glass to usher along those slobbering, greedy, obese, corn syrup-addicted children because, you know, you're worried about their health so you don't want them grouping together?

It's likely you do, so there's no point making a big deal out of it. We mean, look, if you went to all the trouble of obtaining a tube without thinking about whether your house has the proper layout for a candy slide, then you have bigger problems.

It turns out the tube thing is a lot of work, so despite the fact that our neighborhood looked like an oil refinery on Halloween from all this stuff, our house chose not to succumb to this weird Stepford peer pressure business. Besides, what are all these fools going to do with the leftover tubes?

Garbage day (which is supposedly really recycling / compost / waste pickup day, but I'm skeptical about what happens to all that material after it's hauled off) is tomorrow, and I bet we see thousands, *thousands* of those PVC tubes awkwardly propped up next to everyone's cans, not unlike the way moisture-less former Christmas trees are set out for pickup during the weeks following the holiday season, cast aside as if they never meant anything…a dagger to the heart, as it not only symbolizes the end of the spiritual rewards one receives in the form of tons of presents during this time, but also serves as a teasing reminder that Presidents' Day is anywhere from 8 to 8.325 agonizing weeks away, and we all just have to patiently wait, eagerly anticipating the forthcoming pageantry, wine tasting, and generally completely immersive, experiential activities that make it the #1 Holiday of the Year in This Country.

Right behind Halloween.

TRULY CREATIVE PROBLEM-SOLVING

FALL 2020

I s it so wrong to think of hiring an agent just for the sake of having an agent?

Recently I hired this Realtor® to walk into a business meeting with me. When asked who she was, I simply replied, "My agent."

What's the big deal? She is. I mean, she still thinks I'm selling my house, which is totally untrue so she's going to be pissed, but I needed an agent to intimidate someone, so I hired one.

Honestly, she did a terrible job. She kept looking around the room all confused, asking, "What are we talking about?" about a million times, and even got up to leave. Christ! What are you doing, lady? Real agents don't leave meetings unless their rock star client is so over-the-edge he's going to kill somebody, and they don't want to be a witness.

Anyway, I call this temporary agent-hiring of mine Truly Creative Problem-Solving. I added it as a skill on my LinkedIn profile.

You should have seen these fools squirm behind their Gucci face shields. They thought they were going to be able to tell me what to do. But no. No! I told them what to do. With my agent.

Telling people what to do = victory. This is why so many people get into management: #1, to work at a place that has a fridge; #2, to tell people what to do so you achieve victory through your paycheck.

Sometimes there's a #3 that revolves around making positive change through progressive organizational development, but I really think it's mostly about the fridge and paycheck.

Anyway, these tools in their Prada gear looked absolutely terrified of Beverly despite her frazzled behavior. I didn't even have to say a whole lot; I just produced my poutiest gaze at this ridiculous gaggle of Senior Vice Presidents and nodded my head at an awkwardly slow rate every time they spoke. Like really slow, to the point you'd think I might be having a seizure or something. Eventually even Beverly was so entranced by my antics she couldn't help but stay to see what would happen next. Which is saying a lot; Realtors® have the attention spans of gnats due to their constant need to find "paying clients."

Have you ever tried the awkwardly slow head nod? It's the best! It obviously implies, according to cultural mores, a "yes" or "supplication," but the disturbingly slow pace is the equivalent of spraying nerve gas in your enemy's face; they get so confused and have no idea where you stand! Ultimately, they'll just want you to leave, so *boom* you're off the hook for the money you owe and next thing you know you're eating a delicious raspberry scone at a European-ish café and hoping to bum a smoke from that guy who looks like he may have venereal disease.

And you won't have to deal with your agent any longer after this either. Once the whole "sorry, there's no home sale thing happening" is out of the bag, she'll be done with you for sure.

That's what happened during my meeting.

Bonus tip: When you're having a terrible phone call and it's hard and awkward and you're getting yelled at because you don't do your job and you're scared, tip the balance of power in your favor by going completely silent. Totally silent. Not even breathing.

Eventually, the unjust other person will start asking if you're there or if you're listening or whatever, but their harsh tone will automatically lessen in fervor, which is already to your advantage, but right when they start to say, "Hey, [insert your name here], are you listening?" — right at the "are" part — just start talking from the midpoint of a sentence. It totally ruins the whole conversation! It's so great.

Also, and this is important, you need that midpoint sentence preestablished, otherwise you'll choke like you did in Little League and you'll never get that moment back and it will haunt your professional life because you refuse to go to cognitive psychotherapy about ritual humiliation. My favorite midpoint sentence is… are you ready? Now say this with authority, real authority, like The Rock:

"…cross-functionally…outreach, content generation, link-building, onsite and offsite optimizations! And now!"

Am I right or what? I mean, what would you say if someone pulled this on you? Don't answer that; I know. It would be "I need a napkin" because you just spilled your $6.35 chai latte all over your keyboard since you got played by a subordinate like a sucker. Maybe you'd even want that savvy devil to be your new Regional Manager…and offer them a raise.

So that's the lesson. I was going to give you more details about the scandal that led to that meeting, but now that's beside the point. This turned into a free tutorial on Creative Problem-Solving. Now you're ready for all the perks of Management.

REMEDIAL MATHEMATICS

Do you think T-shirts should cost $5.00 apiece? I think at Costco a six-pack of Calvin Klein V-neck T-shirts (I love V-necks, much to the frustration of the general public) costs $30.00.

What would happen if we all paid $30.00 per T-shirt at Costco? I'm a whiz at pivot tables in Excel, so the function tells me the total would be $180.00.

I have roughly 28 T-shirts, as inventoried this morning. Do I need 28 T-shirts? It is my dress of choice, especially on formal occasions. But I could do without. Looking at the detritus of my house, I think this would save a lot of space.

No! Even writing that makes me cringe; I'm an addict, a consumer addict. I need all of these shirts despite the fact that I don't wear 33% of them. I want wearable cotton-based products coursing through my veins. I'm like a starving hyena, desperate for consumer-packaged goods to satisfy my desires. Don't touch my stuff. It's mine's.

Okay, if they cost $30.00 each I'd definitely have at least 50% fewer, and I think at this price they could be manufactured domestically instead of through international slave labor. So that means jobs. And less waste. And a shrinkage of the floating plastic island in the Pacific Ocean that young person is trying to clean up with a giant net. I saw it on *60 Minutes*.

But what about my other stuff? I'd go broke trying to replace it all in order to feel good. Sweatshirts (another classy staple), multiple dress shirts of which I wear one approximately once a year, jeans, sweats, slacks of a sort, socks, (no underwear, I skip that), baseball hats, stocking caps…

You know how many tumblers are in my cupboard? About 117. There's like five Swig® tumblers, a host of coffee ones, and mysterious plastic-metal hybrids that are of the "sport" variety, even though if I participated in a sport right now my priority would be orchestrating super long time-outs so I could eat chips and drink Mountain Dew.

What if all this stuff suffered a 500% price increase, which is what the internet says is the percentage increase from $5.00 to $30.00?

Would China resort to military tactics to maintain dominance?

Would I become depressed?

Would I suddenly find the time to review basic mathematics?

Would there be an appropriate and necessary redistribution of wealth in our country?

It's like last night's presidential debate. I already knew what was going to happen, yet I didn't want to know.

BLACK MIRROR REDUX

WINTER 2020

I haven't seen *Black Mirror* but I believe the first episode of the first season concludes with something about the Prime Minister of England, a pig, and a nationally televised broadcast.

What would be awesome is if, when faced with the gruesome task forced upon him to save the Royal Family kidnappee, the Prime Minister just says, "Okay, great!" Then kind of hesitates and asks, "Wait, you mean right now? Are you going to stay here in the room?"

And the perpetrator guy kind of looks upset at the lack of effect he's having, then somewhat horrified that the Prime Minister seems so unfazed by the whole thing, so he repeats the sadistic instructions in case maybe the Prime Minister misheard him or something. But nope, he understands what I'm asking him, this guy's a real weirdo it turns out. Plus is it just me or does he seem kind of dumb? Sweet Jesus, this guy's technically in charge of our nuclear missile program. I'm going to be sick. Let's just slowly backpedal out of here and I'll go back to my Account Executive day job. I should make an appearance anyway; I haven't been in all week.

And the Prime Minister goes about his dirty business, somewhat deadpan but kind of whistling a jaunty tune as if he's washing dishes. Maybe an Adele song. Something really irritating so the viewer loses sympathy for the Prime Minister and subsequently finds themself rooting for the evil mastermind, maybe understanding that the life of a storied Account Executive is really stressful and could likely drive any of us into barbarous mayhem.

But again I haven't seen it because it seems so weird, and thus I've likely messed up some of the details in this alternate ending. I've also heard you should never whistle in prison as it makes people really mad.

RING AROUND THE RING

It turns out there's a whole community behind the Ring Video Doorbell installed on my front door.

Well, it's next to my front door.

You don't know where I live, unless you also have a Ring Video Doorbell and are familiar with the secret side button double-click that generates a map of all other Ring Video Doorbell enthusiasts' exact location across the greater continental United States, including address, phone number, secret phone number, and credit score.

If you lack a Ring Video Doorbell, your other method of locating me (or anyone) is based on whether you have a 21st-Century Child, for if you do, this Child could undoubtedly scroll some binary code faster than I eat a chicken wing and provide you with my exact weight, height, address, and susceptibility to phishing schemes — all based on the middle three letters of my last name.

But since you don't know where I live because I can tell neither of these options apply to you, I'm very comfortable pointing out that my Ring Video Doorbell is not hard-wired to my house and thus is as easy to steal as the freshly delivered, barely recyclable UPS package on my front porch.

It's just sitting on a screw. The Ring. I didn't even install the screw — the screw came with the house.

You'd want my Ring Video Doorbell. What it does is…well, when you press the button it makes a ring noise, like the doorbell you grew up with. Or when you walk by, it kind of scans you and sends an X-ray to the National Security Agency, also like the doorbell you grew up with. Oh and your phone beeps, etc., when either of these things happen. So you know when you have a visitor or walker-by-er. Or possibly an intruder, which would be bad, and is why I'm currently pitching Ring International Pricing Concern, LTD, on my idea of a Ring Exploding Video Doorbell. But so far no contract attorney or industrial engineer will take my case/project, despite the promise of a lucrative payment at an undetermined future date.

Along with providing ringing noises and security, the Ring Video Doorbell has this propensity for recording the ludicrous behavior of squirrels during the day (what a life!), possums during the night, any car that drives by no matter the Ring's distance to the street or how many times you've messed with the settings, and your neighbors' various antics.

The neighbor thing is really interesting. For example, I receive unsolicited electronic communiqués from my Ring app in the form of "neighborhood alerts"…

[I think they call them this for the same reason CNN overused the "Terror Alert Level" in the early 2000s — that Green-Blue-Yellow-Orange-Red/low-to-high anticipated violence thermometer — without explaining that the system was never intended to go lower than yellow: to scare the holy bejeezus out of us so we'd watch more.]

…that include fascinating, albeit brief anecdotes from people I don't know, including this notice:

> Stolen chair – Person took chair and tried to depart in loud pickup truck. I was able to chase down truck and recover the chair. (Accompanied by a blurry "before" shot of a backyard patio set, less one chair, followed by a clearer "after" shot, plus one chair.)

This begs the question of whether the retail value of the hijacked chair was remotely worth

the physical harm that could befall a homeowner
in the speedy pursuit of a possibly armed cat
burglar escaping at a hasty, likely reckless
speed in the middle of the night in an attempt
to reach the Main Hideout with the coveted
prize of that single non-Adirondack chair.

The real question here is, how brave is this
homeowner? That's the juice. I mean come on
storyteller guy, you can't leave that part out.
Don't be coy.

Did you dive into the back of the truck, grab
the chair, and combat-roll out the other side?
Did you attach yourself to the hood of the
truck à la *Raiders of the Lost Ark* and have an
extended fight scene that included you almost
getting knocked to your death but instead you
were able to use your bullwhip to attach
yourself to the undercarriage and…?

"Nope. I'm good. I just recovered the chair.
Nothing more to say. Just another day in the
life of a Real Hero."

Maybe the human homeowner didn't do any of
this.

Maybe The Ring did it all, communicating with
other supposedly inanimate things like in that
movie *Heavy Metal* where the cars come to life.
That makes more sense and at least explains the
unreasonable amount of humility my fellow Ring
Owner displays. I bet The Ring communicated
with a Dodge Challenger that rammed the thief's

truck, got the chair back, and returned it to its rightful owner.

Either way, I want to get rid of my Ring. It's leaving me vulnerable to judgement and scrutiny. I mean, what are people seeing in my neighborhood alert?

Unshowered homeowner goes to mini-mart, returns with beer and gum.

Car prowler extremely disappointed after discovering nothing of value in man's Subaru.

Man accidentally picks nose in front of neighbor during early morning dog walk.

Yes, I think I've about had it with this thing. If you want a free Ring, just come on by and grab it. You already know where I live.

CONNECTING THE
CONNECTION REQUEST

SPRING 2020

Does anyone get their LinkedIn Friend, er, Connection Request rejected?

It must happen.

Perhaps it's done in a passive-aggressive way, where the recipient of the request kind of curls up into a ball, shrinks back from the desk, and powers down their laptop with one curled finger rather than say "no."

Is there even a "no" option? Someone send me a Friend, er, Connection Request and I'll see if there's some form of rejection button.

If there is an outright rejection option, that would be SO GREAT and add an element of humanity to The World's Foremost Professional Gatherer of Studio Headshots Completely Unrepresentative of the

Current State of the User.

And I mean crushing rejection, like the time in the sixth grade when Susan Carlyle told me she didn't want to hold my hand because I was Catholic.

LinkedIn is a mystery. The times I've spoken to people about it (people I know, and physically see, who happen to be employed), the discussion turns to its (a) "crappy" communication format, (b) tendency to generate unwanted solicitations (not for me — I'm desperate for solicitations), and (c) accumulation of connections that end up being people you don't actually know.

This latter part I can attest to. Frequently I'll look for some company to extort and next to the organization's name there's this teeny tiny circle with an image in it and the phrase "1 connection works here." What? I have no idea who that person is. Do I owe her money? Can I ask her for money? Is she susceptible to Ponzi schemes? I'll never know, because I don't know. Them.

I'm assuming this same disassociated association exists on popular social media platforms that I don't utilize because I don't want people knowing my business. Like Facebook. Or Instagram. (Truth be told, I avoid Instagram because I take terrible selfies that scream "Catholic," which I'm still traumatized about thanks to Susan.)

I'm sure LinkedIn makes sense and I'm just misunderstanding it and reinforcing this misunderstanding by only surrounding myself with dysfunctional, slightly out of shape, middle-aged people who also think the Internet is an elaborate trick.

In the meantime I've hired a photographer to help me glam up my profile picture.

TOM BRADY CAME CLOSE TO RUINING YOUR LIFE, YOU JUST DIDN'T KNOW IT

WINTER 2021

I'm about two years older than Tom Brady. Maybe three or four. Okay, I don't know exactly, and you know what? I don't want to know.

I do know that my friend and I were most definitely not rooting for Tom and the Tampa Bay Buccaneers during last Sunday's Divisional Playoff Game. And, by proxy, not rooting for Rob Gronkowski. But really, really, with lots of strained effort and creased foreheads, not rooting for Tom.

With Gronkowski it's because of his previous massive, unstoppable success, coupled with a jock-ish/oaf vibe. However, my unresearched understanding is, while incredibly accomplished and potentially oafish in nature, "Gronk" is actually quite pleasant, supportive, and fun-loving. Like he'd make a great neighbor.

Imagine how much he could help you when it comes to moving in new furniture or adding a nice deck to your house. He could just pick up the entire platform upon completion and walk it wherever you want. Even if it's to a new town.

Ah, Gronk's likely a good human being. More's the pity.

With Tom, the anti-rooting is a function not of visceral hatred but rather complete and utter alienation. He's alienating. Those chiseled features. Supermodel wife. Nice house(s). Incredible ability to still perform at the highest level as an NFL quarterback despite the unspecified but certainly proximal nature of our ages (I get sore just from riding a spin bike for 20 minutes). Plus, I hear from unsubstantiated sources that Tom, like Gronkowski, is actually a nice (albeit unusually competitive) person. I bet even his kids are kind little humans already. Not spray-painting profanities on my neighbor's car like my kid.

See? Alienating. And I haven't even gotten to the world of measurement. You know, that mental world where we compare ourselves to, say, our neighbor with the bigger house, newer car, and misdemeanor-free children and we subsequently feel bad and thus eat an entire bag of Doritos in hopes of generating just a little bit of joy in our lives. I guess in layman's terms this phenomenon of comparison (excluding the

Doritos) is called "keeping up with the Joneses."

So, yes, Tom Brady officially alienates all football-watching men older than 40. Excluding men in Boston and Tampa Bay. It's a scientific fact. And this alienation is exacerbated by the keeping-up-with-the-Joneses effect where (in the Tom vs. Me paradigm) I think to myself, "I'm 40-something and worth _____ and I have _____ and run a 15-minute mile, but TOM is 40-something-slightly-less-than-me and has mansions and a net worth of (oh my God I looked it up) $200 million and really nice, straight teeth, plus the other stuff we already talked about."

So I rooted against him last weekend. And I will root against him when he plays Green Bay this coming Sunday. But wait, what about Aaron Rodgers? He has all the same stuff — rumored kindness, great sense of humor, incredible talent, piles, big piles, huge piles of hundred-dollar bills he sleeps on every night. What separates the two? Why am I picking on Tom?

Oh. I know.

I'm a Seahawks fan.

Now you're just going to say, "Hey, you're still upset about Super Bowl XCVD&%%LLVV" or whichever one was the one where the Seahawks lost to the Patriots at the very end part. And while I follow your logic, and indeed that unmentionable event I just mentioned still sears my psyche like a red-hot poker, I'm here to tell you how wrong you are. Especially if you're from Boston. Boston people are always wrong.

I'm officially not rooting for Tom Brady because behind the gapless-toothed smile and strong but soft-skinned handshakes lies the worst example of good sportsmanship ever to exist in this galaxy. That's right, I'm talking about the February 9, 2015, Great Grammy Awards Scandal of Meanness.

It was eight days after Super Bowl 49. I was curled up in my favorite soft, plush Garfield blanket, rocking back and forth, trying to forget that last-second goal line interception, eating my fourth box of See's Candies, watching the 57th Grammy Awards…and there, to my horror, trotted out "Tonight's Special Guests" to present the Award for Best Rock Album. None other than Malcolm Butler, Julian Edelman, and… TOM BRADY.

Imagine sitting on your couch, innocently enjoying your favorite snack, mindlessly absorbing a vapid television program, when suddenly a Great White Shark crashes through your window and eats your face. That's what this felt like.

The worst part is the trio actually did a really good job presenting the award. Made some solid jokes. Entertained the masses. Beautifully intersected sports celebrity with musical celebrity. It was seamless…almost like an experienced signal-caller had orchestrated the whole thing, not unlike his two final (touchdown-pass-producing) drives during Super Bowl 49. Hmmmm…who has that kind of preternatural talent?

That's right, I mean it's off the radar, and people likely think some Producer or Key Grip made that Grammy broadcast "so special," but I know it was Tom. His fingerprints are all over it. And for that extremely unsportsmanlike stab in the heart of all Seahawks fans everywhere, for that virtual noogie, for that act of kicking us while we were down, for that I cannot in good conscience react like a mature or well-adjusted adult. No, for that betrayal, I must root against Tom Brady. Not necessarily forever, but necessarily this weekend against Aaron Rodgers and the Green Bay Packers. And forever after that.

I realize you likely don't care. Unless, possibly, you're a Seahawks fan (i.e., extraordinarily intelligent, attractive, and otherwise perfect).

And that's the great thing about sports. The act of watching a given event is not unlike playing a video game: It turns your mind off, allowing you to actively relax, similar to the way the Great White Shark who ate my face sleeps. And even though my team's not in the NFC Championship game this year, and even though I still can't bear to watch that interception or think about Tom Brady cruising down the highway in a convertible with the wind playfully tossing his coiffed hair around, I'll be watching football this weekend, because I have a singular, very important reason.

And I get the feeling I always will.

SEVENTH-GRADE NEWSROOM BRAWL

FALL 2020

Have you heard those stories about Australian rugby teams being on international flights and they have their uniforms on or at least red-and-white horizontal-striped long-sleeved shirts with grass stains and blood all over and they're already drunk then they just keep partying and getting more drunk and somehow the flight attendants and all the passengers are cool with it although when I try to party like that on a plane I at best get scolded and/or told I'm a "travesty" or at worst forcibly detained by a sky marshal in the gross lavatory?

Then, as the rugby team story goes, the next thing you know the whole section of the cabin they've taken over is doing that arm-in-arm, swaying-embrace chain thing and singing good ol' Australian soccer or football or whatever ballads and the team has plied the entire plane with beer and lo and behold there's the captain partying too but it's cool 'cause he hit the autopilot button? And everyone just gets wasted? And the entire plane has total patience with the outright brawls that spontaneously erupt amongst the players every thirty seconds simply because they're lovable Australians?

Have you heard about this? I believe it. I've heard about it.

At least once. Or possibly I saw it in a movie. Or maybe I dreamt it.

Speaking of which, I once dreamt I was driving a Ferrari. The original *Magnum P.I.* from-the-'80s kind you can now buy for like 22 grand. Did you know Tom Selleck was a big-time heartthrob in the '80s? My friend's mom told my friend this fairly recently, and he told me. Which is weird now that I think about it.

Anyway, in my dream my Ferrari kept stalling because I couldn't figure out how to shift gears (Ferraris have gated shifting, so you have to finesse it just right to make the shaft move through the slots). Then I saw on the *Today Show* before it became creepy (it had Jane Pauley back then; she's decidedly uncreepy) that in dreams cars symbolize your life. Which was highly discouraging to hear since it obviously implied I didn't know how to move my life forward.

The point is quite obvious — Australian rugby teams getting 200 airline passengers plus the crew wasted gives us hope. And with hope, we can eviscerate our worst enemy: the mundane, which is the #1 cause of not being able to move our lives forward.

We need to examine the mundane and make it interesting. Take job descriptions. Look closely…they seem somehow threatening. That's right, threatening. Try it out, right now. It's like the job poster assumes you're planning a felony on your first day.

What else is mundane? Oh, anyone who talks about their work. They launch into these bizarre spiels in coded language about the mission and the role and the oh please stop speaking now and let's party with some beer, okay?

How about mind-numbing local news? At least there are attractive anchorpeople to look at — they have incredible hair, the men and women both. I wonder if they have get-togethers and when everyone shows up at the traffic reporter's condo they're all somehow perfectly coiffed like during the 9:00 p.m. news. And they probably DON'T DRINK at these things since they're worried about the extra pounds the camera adds. So there's lots of celery available. And water. And they talk about…what do they talk about? Oh, other anchors, of course.

It's like junior high all over again. They absolutely have to spend the majority of their social time making fun of different channels' news teams. I bet they prank them too — like call during the news hour to let the live anchors know that they have a piece of celery in their teeth. Or that they're fat. At least that's what I'd do if I were a news anchor. Maybe not the fat thing; that's pretty mean. Fortunately for society I'm scared of teleprompters and rouge, so we don't have to worry about this anymore.

I forgot what we were talking about.

Oh! Right. Bettering our lives by exploding the mundane. That's the theme. Not being boring. Next time you're traveling, or working, or doing whatever, pretend you're on an Australian rugby team and have a beer or spritzer or whatever for me, in your best un-mundane way.

SNOW-COVERED BIGOTRY

T he snow was, quite mysteriously, very cold on our feet for some reason.

We had nice big snow boots on. And snow pants that made us (okay, just me) look fat. It's the pants' fault entirely, not at all my body's fault. A really good gig would be to invent snow pants that make moderately unfit, mature individuals look skinny.

We also had multiple-pound-producing, puffy, snow-worthy coats on. And hats that made our (okay fine, my) hair look bad.

But our feet were still universally cold.

Sledding off a side road in the Olympic Mountains is not for the faint of heart. It's not the wilderness component or hypothermia potential or roving packs of wild deer that makes it dangerous. It's the people you meet.

For example, this seven-foot-tall unshaven man in quite a hurry appeared out of the woods with his wolf dog. I couldn't possibly imagine why he was in a hurry other than my concern that he had just buried a body, or maybe he just didn't like fat-looking people. He appeared to be quite comfortable in the woods though, so I kind of kept an eye on where he was going in case the deer attacked.

I guess we didn't technically meet this wilderness man though. We did meet an interesting blonde-only family consisting of a husband, wife, and 900 little blonde kids. Like all blonde families they arrived on-site in a shiny new SUV. The kids piled out screaming and covered in chocolate like a 21st-century version of the von Trapps, minus the penchant for bursting into song and cavorting around in Bavarian dance.

As the happy, hyperglycemic elves began sledding with our children, the Patriarch kind of ambled up to us, playfully stirring the snow with his $877.00 Lands' End All-Weather Boots like a farmer taking a break from building a fence and talking to his buddies about the weather…or possibly a baseball player calling time-out supposedly to adjust his cup but in reality he's just messing with the pitcher, which I think should be illegal because baseball games just take too long and all of these antics make me groan at the prospect of sitting through yet another five-hour pitchers' duel, despite the wide availability of lite beer.

Anyway, the Leader eventually starts talking about the local area and how they moved here from California to be with "like-minded people." At first I thought he simply meant "also really good-looking people," so I was both pleased and kind of surprised that our attractiveness was so evident despite our protuberant snowsuits.

But after gauging my encouraged, possibly beaming expression, he chose to read my physiological response to what I thought was gross, cheap, completely self-involved flattery as some kind of signal that I also, and therefore we also, preferred only the company of white people, to the degree that we sought to surround ourselves only with white people and bathe in the glory of being white people while speaking disparagingly of nonwhite people.

Indeed, the rest of the conversation involved me kind of standing there with my mouth open, then averting my eyes and toying with the snow, using my boot tip to buy time like those frustrating baseball players, while this fellow proceeded to describe a hero's journey from the depths of Mexican-filled California to the idyllic landscape of the Olympic Peninsula, with its incredible vistas, affordable property, and acres of whites.

It turns out there is kind of a surreal, out-of-body experience that transpires when one meets a fairly avid racist on an idyllic, albeit unsanctioned sledding hill in the Olympic Mountains. I sort of floated above the pine trees for a while as a Yanni cassette played in my head to drown out his voice. Then everything crashed back down to snow-covered Mother Earth, and I vaguely recall mentioning that I had chronic diarrhea and that I and my white family and friends (one of whom actually hails from South America, not sure if he caught that) definitely had to get going very quickly right now posthaste. Stop crying, kids, we're leaving.

To be fair, this gentleman was far cagier than I'm implying here. He was subtle and suggestive, like a career politician hyper-adept at making claims in such a way that they could never be used in rebuttal or for an opponent's campaign purposes. But the whole thing was super weird and tragic and interesting, and you just don't know what is going to happen anywhere at any time. Especially in the mountains.

SAVE YOUR QUARTERS

WINTER 2021

I've written about enterprising neighborhood capitalists before...

...Did you see that? The little blue link thing? It won't work here, but it's an online tool you may not be familiar with called Search Engine Optimization, or "SEO" for short. It's pronounced "see-yo" conversationally. Whenever I interview for writing jobs in one of the 44,832 technology companies here in the Pacific Northwest, I'm always peppering my very one-way conversation (I really can't quite emphasize how much I get carried away when talking about myself; I typically request a mirror halfway through the interview, and by the end I typically forget why I'm even there) with frequent see-yo's to demonstrate my "domain knowledge" (another industry catchphrase that indicates my superior knowledge and general deservingness of said job) to impress the interviewee. Ah, interviewer. Who for some reason always seems to be frowning or in a hurry to get out of there.

Some of my other favorite industry or "I am a professional person worthy of very important meetings" jargon includes "product market fit," "hive mind," and "bullet point" because these phrases create this void where hopefully the listener struggles to follow the conversation and therefore I win.

Oh, and if young people are around I use "Damn, it feels good to be a gangster" because it makes me relevant and similarly young-seeming, when the truth is I've started to make grunting noises when I bend my knees beyond a 45-degree angle.

All of this begs the question: Is the usage of acronyms and industry jargon an acquired habit or innate instinct? If it's the former, is there anything we can do to stop this? If it's the latter, does that make one an insufferable douche?

So these eight-year-old neighborhood capitalists were literally hiding in their playhouse next to the sidewalk where I was walking my faithful dog, Woofums. Not true. His name is Benji. I've always wanted to get a dog and name him "Woofums" though, and get a cat and name him "Dog," and get a bird and name him "Bald-Ass Monkey." Okay, also not true, I'm not a big bird fan since as a child my friends (okay, friend) who had birds were always saying things like "Don't get too close, he'll bite you, he's really mean." Which sounds like a really unpleasant trait in a pet and begs the question as to why they owned a bird in the first place. Maybe the bird learned it from my friends, er, friend, because secretly my friend was super mean and bit people. Either way it'd be super fun to say, "Here's your birdseed or worms or whatever, Bald-Ass Monkey!"

Anyway, the capitalists were hiding in this dilapidated playhouse while I was walking the dog and looking into my neighbors' windows. Wait. I mean, do you look in your neighbors' windows? I try to avoid it, but since it gets dark very early here in The Great Pacific Raining Northwest (why do people keep moving here?), people's windows light up like 10,000-watt searchlights by 3:00 p.m. and this sort of draws me to accidentally look inside their homes. I literally have to consciously focus on the sidewalk or straight ahead or completely vertically, which looks ridiculous, in order to avoid these spotlit windows. I swear I don't do it all the time or really ever, but this morning I saw movement in one window and lo and behold there's the neighbor kid eating breakfast or whatever and his head snaps up like one of those fast zombies from *28 Days Later* (resisted urge to use SEO there) and he looks at me like I'm some criminal pervert.

Which I'm not. Ugh, walking the dog is so stressful.

Right before the capitalists attacked, I saw a form in this two-million-dollar house that just sold (please stop moving to Seattle) and I really wanted to see the person behind the form so I could appropriately judge them as horrible for having so much money and possibly introduce myself so I could look better by having rich friends although I'd never invite them over to my sub-million-dollar home. As nice as it is.

But the capitalists, luckily I guess, interrupted my attempted snooping and offered to "…draw lines, or abstract art…" for a mere ten cents. The nerve! I told them I didn't have any  money and they should be in school, at which point they offered to do it for FREE. What kind of capitalists are you? Definitely need more education. But it turns out they "took me to school" (another catchphrase I use around young people at work — if I had a job — in order to be relevant…they just eat it up) because after receiving the artwork (I ordered abstract art, but still just got lines, albeit kind of squiggly lines emanating from the center of the page à la a supernova…probably a metaphor for hope in these trying times), I found myself offering a form of reverse layaway by quickly saying I'd come right back and pay them a

QUARTER. So clever. Those conniving eight-year-olds should be in charge of a tech company — they purposefully engineered the whole transaction to make me come back, the act of which they monetized at like 3876% or whatever fifteen cents over a dime is, exactly the same process created by those creepy engineers who designed the app your psyche is so desperately telling you to take a pull from rather than read this ravishing exposé.

The point of this is I'm out a quarter, and be careful where you walk. Some people are trying to bust you looking into their windows so they can call the police and collect a reward, while others are getting you addicted to stuff they can profit from. That's why from here on out the dog will have to run on the treadmill, and all future pets will be fish. Two fish, to be exact. One will be named "Goat," the other "Rabbit."

I LOVE GETTING HUSTLED

WINTER 2021

The space-time continuum vacuum we're all currently existing in thanks to the virus, made all the more surreal thanks to the *Mad Max 2: The Road Warrior*—styled bandits attempting to overthrow the federal government on January 6th, has led to a proliferation of professional development courses, particularly of the online variety.

Okay, that's not fair. They were more like Mongol Hordes than Lord Humungus's marauders. That's right! The main bad guy in *Mad Max 2: The Road Warrior* goes by "Lord Humungus." I'm going to change my LinkedIn name to that.

And I have nothing against Mongol Hordes, take it easy. They're just one of history's prominent examples of mass invaders, so it kind of came to mind real

quick. Besides, I've always wanted to join a horde, they seem so motivated and supportive. And yes, it's true, I can change my LinkedIn name to anything I want and you can't stop me. It will probably lead to tons of job offers. Especially after I tell the recruiter I actually played Lord Humungus in *Mad Max 2: The Road Warrior*. It turns out on the Internet you can tell people anything and they'll believe you because everyone's in such a frenetic rush to find facts for their story, avoid Fear of Missing Out, and/or a buy a product they need instantaneously. When it comes to facts, I mean, when was the last time you backed up research you did online by looking at an actual book or speaking with an accredited scholar of some kind? Books and scholars are doomed.

Plus if the recruiter demands evidence, I'll just show them my physique and hockey mask. If you haven't Googled "Lord Humungus" yet, do it now and you'll see what I mean. Er, maybe Google *Mad Max 2: The Road Warrior*…I have a feeling searching for "Lord Humungus" could lead you somewhere you don't want to go, or possibly to a really disturbing Craigslist ad.

Upon further reflection and an application of baby oil to my chest, it's slightly possible the apparent propagation of online professional development courses is actually a direct result of my searching for them, rather than being caused by catastrophic world events, but I can't be sure.

Why I'm searching for online professional development courses is a private matter, in no way related to the idea that I suddenly realized I may be short of perfect. Professionally. And maybe, technically, I need an income, but that depends on your worldview.

Either way, there's a lot of these courses out there, some created by shady organizations that want my social security number to register, which I gladly provide; others by individual proprietors of sorts. Professional proprietors.

Thus, I smell a hustle. Which I love.

That's right, I love getting hustled. But not dirty, gritty hustled like on the street, which is basically the equivalent of robbery so there's lots of adrenaline involved, mostly related to life endangerment. No, no, I prefer nice, safe Internet hustling. It's a fascinating process.

For example, I signed up for a "free" (I think the marketing term for "free" is the ominous phrase "demand generation") course about effectively condensing what amounts to a slightly long-range professional goal-setting exercise onto one sheet of paper.

The pitch, er, course began with an overly dramatic before-and-after story involving a gentleman who went from working 60 hours a week without vacation, having massive credit card debt, and owing back taxes to adding $650,000 in "revenue" (not sure how), paying off all his debt and taxes, becoming fire chief, and taking his wife on a two-week cruise — all without trafficking in heroin, all within one year.

Then we went through a process where we were supposed to raise our hands if we suffered various ailments or common human conditions encapsulated by catchphrases like "analysis paralysis," "productivity rollercoaster," and so on and so forth.

At which point I realized this was exactly like a class I happened to stay awake for in college (they refuse to admit I'm an alumnus, which is fine as I don't have money for them) where the professor read horoscopes and had us raise our hands if we thought they applied to us and of course we all just raised our hands constantly and she explained the Barnum effect is a psychological phenomenon whereby individuals give high accuracy ratings to descriptions of their personality that supposedly are tailored specifically to them yet which are in fact vague and somewhat general enough to apply to a wide range of people.

(From "the Barnum effect" onward in the above paragraph is completely and unabashedly plagiarized from Wikipedia; I didn't have time to do other research or validate the definition.)

Also, one time I fell asleep during Fisheries 101 and as the professor demonstrated shore casting, where you use this huge pole to throw a lure out past the breakers, I woke up right before the lure landed in the seat next to me, which if I'd still been asleep would have likely caused me to jump up and scream like a schoolgirl, much to the amusement of my 700 or so fellow students.

That was a close one. As was this online professional development course that I frantically exited out of as fast as my sweaty fingers could mash the keyboard before I started typing phrases like "scam," "run," and "you're getting hustled" in the chat waterfall.

Maybe I should have warned everyone. Or perhaps some folks benefit from this stuff regardless of my take on the grift. Hopefully it works for some people. It's just not for me. Besides, I can always fall back on my acting career.

THE FUTURE WILL NOT INVOLVE UNDERWEAR

We should all do time capsules about this whole pandemic thing. As in a steel tube approximately one foot long with a 4.25-inch diameter buried 20 feet underground, in my case filled with various writings. Oh, and several headshots as I want to be famous in the distant future, like 500 years from now. Five hundred years is an important delineation — haven't you noticed what a snoozefest history any time after 500 years ago is? I mean, who really wants to know about something that happened 418 years ago? The math alone is impossible to do.

Some of the headshots will be taken at jaunty angles, others will be themed "Hats from Around the World," and a final set will involve my special pursed-lip pose. Mark your calendar: me famous in 2020 + 500 =_____. In the future someone will be able to do that math, so it's fine to not understand it today.

But I don't want to be famous now, not now. Now would be bad as I have several sets of wild accusations submitted from which I'm trying to derive an income. Not extortion or bullying or threats or blackmail or anything actually criminal or damaging. Just wild accusations submitted to whomever in various mediums, i.e., I verbally accused my neighbor Craig of replacing my matte black 2020 Mercedes Benz S-450 4MATIC Sedan with a 2006 Subaru Forester, albeit the L.L. Bean edition. So far Craig's only response has been "Get out of my yard."

So when we make our time capsules, don't think you're just doing this to meet a requirement or get extra credit or become involved in arts and crafts (ugh, arts and crafts rooms have a particular smell which I detest, somewhere between mildew/fabric softener/chamomile tea and old-people skin). No, these will have a real impact on the 12-foot-tall, no-underwear-wearing People of the Future, because when these big-headed giants open up our steel tube they may be concerned they'll get the virus — but then they'll realize they won't because it will be dead. Just like when you open a World War II time capsule you don't catch Nazism or belief in the Greater East Asian Co-Prosperity Sphere, or think discrimination within the military makes sense.

You probably don't know how to move forward with your capsule, so here's an example of what I'll document for today, 5/27/2020:

Hello, Space Giants of the Future. Patrick McNerthney here; feel free to grab an autographed headshot from the pile. Today, because of a pandemic where most of the world is forced to stay inside their homes and work (or look for work; the economics of this outbreak are pretty grim) – all while educating their children, if they have children – my day involved attempting to work and look for more work while homeschooling my son.

Specifically, this meant trying not to yell at my kid as he interrupted me with legitimate questions during "school," trying not to yell at my kid when he told me he was finished with his schoolwork (11:00 a.m.; he started at 9:00 a.m.), making lunch for the both of us, and forcing him to go on a bike ride to offset his lack of access to recess, sports, and other physical activity, particularly in light of the mutually agreed upon two-hour Fortnite gaming time allotted to him each day.

Then I kept trying to work while he played Fortnite – which, admittedly, involved me yelling at him a lot because he was yelling into his microphoned headset at his friends who were also online playing Fortnite, which is ridiculous because the whole point of a microphoned headset is to amplify your voice while experiencing an insulated audial capture of other sound. All of which you know well, what with your surgically-implanted-at-birth voice amplifiers and Beats by Dre Powerbeats3 headphones.

Two points of clarification: "Fortnite" was a shooting game kids loved in 2020 that was eventually outlawed because it made them clinically insane. "Online" was a relatively new medium where humans connected with each other through a series of transistors in vacuum tubes wired together (thus on-line) and spread across the globe — also eventually outlawed when it became apparent it was entirely controlled by one credit card company. And, ironically, because when combined with a thing called a "mobile phone," it led to the human race losing the ability to verbally communicate with one another face to face in real time. Something that's probably hard to understand now as you undoubtedly control time with your laser fingers.

Okay, maybe I should not be the one doing a time capsule as surely recapping the events of my day will lull our future jet-boot-wearing readers into a deep slumber. But you should do one for sure.

I better go check on my kid.

LONGER

HOW TO HOST A COCAINE PARTY SHOOT-OUT

SUMMER 2020

I t would be great to invite your friends over to your vacation rental, then create a fake death scene before they arrive.

There are some important keys to this gag though.

First, the vacation rental needs to be an actual vacation rental and not your house; i.e., it's not in the town you live in, you have to actually travel to get there, so I guess I'm saying it's somewhat remote or at least has large setbacks between neighboring homes. This lessens the likelihood of police being involved and of your friends reacting to the scene with extreme, panicked violence, since they'll be in that "we're on vacation" relaxed mode. It also ensures you stay committed; we think it would be easier for you to chicken out if you tried this in your own home. Don't ask who "we" is (are?), just know we're in the tree across the street watching you read this, unless you live in the desert or the North Pole or the ocean or Anaheim. All of which notably lack trees, within which we like to hide.

Also, traveling to get to the place of the murder scene (and ensuing hilarity) adds a level of mystery and excitement to this completely immersive experience, we decided.

Next, you need to prepare something crazy elaborate, yet plausible. We learned it's not cool to throw fake blood on the driveway and lie on your side with ground hamburger next to your head and your clothes all torn up, then place a taxidermized Bengal tiger in the bushes complete with menacing, growling soundtrack to simulate a carnivorous attack. It's just not believable and people end up laughing at you because they know Bengal tigers are not native to North America so at best it's an (implausible) zoo-escape scenario…and this leaves you super pissed at the laughing so you tell them to leave and to "please give me my wallet back."

We think you should do this:

Buy a bunch of guns, preferably on the Internet so you have to meet the seller downtown someplace. Then go to your local shooting range and ask for the shell casings. If you ask, "Can I collect some of the brass?" you'll look super cool and "in the know" about guns to the Range Master, who will thus give you the brass. We've always wanted that name, "Range Master." "Hey, everything's gonna be alright, 'Range Master' is here."

Also, buy a dark pair of sunglasses for each member of your family. And some pig blood.

You'll also need:

Rolled-up hundred-dollar bills

Gold chain necklaces

Boom box playing loud speed metal

Credit cards

Ammunition that matches the caliber of your gun

This is going to be great. So when you get to the vacation rental, search for sugar, powdered or otherwise. This would also be a good time to see how many cameras and microphones the perverts who own this place put in the bathrooms. And kitchen.

Now look, we know you're wondering about the pig blood (everybody does) so let's get to it: You're trying to simulate blood spatter. Which means you can't just pour it on the carpet. Take a paintbrush (we told you to buy one, you just forgot) and sort of flick the blood on the walls next to where your family will be lying down to simulate corpses. (Oh. Your family will be lying down to simulate corpses.)

Since everybody but you is dead, there obviously needs to be an area of spatter on the wall for each person.

Then pour the rest of the pig blood on the carpet. And maybe on some of the bedding. Who cares? It's a rental.

Next, pour the sugar in a mountainous pile in the middle of the main dining table, which is hopefully glass — that would be so cool! Then, using a credit card, drag a portion over to each chair. Take about half of each portion and "cut" about 20 "lines." Of those 20 take about 5 to 10 and cut them in halves and/or quarters and either eat the remaining sugar (yum) or push it on the floor or whatever. Next, roll up your hundred-dollar bills (a.k.a. "Benjamins") and put them on the table, making sure to get some of the sugar on the bills so they look "used."

We, ah, heard this is how cocaine parties work. That's what you're simulating.

Put a few of the sunglasses and guns on the table too.

And one of the gold chain necklaces. And a credit card.

Okay, you're doing good. If you have kids and they're crying, tell them you're just playing a new form of Monopoly.

So take the ammunition that fits your gun and put it in the gun. Open the door, shoot your gun once, making sure you're inside the vacation rental, then close the door real quick. You don't have to shoot a hole in the wall, but again we guess you could since this isn't your place. Really we just want the smell of gunfire (technically cordite) inside.

Next, take all the "brass" and throw it all over the room where the blood spatter is. Then, have your family douse themselves in the remaining pig blood and lie down.

(We forgot to mention the timing is important, so do this a maximum of 30 minutes before your guests arrive so you don't get depressed lying around in such a morbid scene.)

You (the reader here — are you still here? — this is so great) are the last one standing (get it?), so you need to hit "Play" on the boom box so the speed metal is really loud. And let the prostitutes in. We forgot to tell you to invite prostitutes over to add a level of realism to your First Ever Cocaine Party Shoot-out Death Scene gag.

Now you lie down. We know you're super excited. Try not to giggle at the hilarity that's about to ensue. Tell your kids to stop crying, this isn't that weird. Nowwwww…here come your guests! See? The prostitutes just let them in! Sob uncontrollably at the loss of your family, you really have to sell it, while they lie still. Remember, you're the only survivor.

Awesome work! Prepare ye for an onslaught of holiday, birthday, and cocktail party invitations; you're officially the talk of the town! Are they laughing? How much do your friends love you right now?

You're welcome.

SEE WHAT YOU'VE BEEN
MISSING

FALL 2020

You may be wondering whether port cities come with seedy underbellies, as implied by the 1980s neon-splashed smash hit series *Miami Vice* (after which I've modeled most of my life).

They do.

The Usual Suspects, Transformers: Revenge of the Fallen, Harry Potter — all take place in port cities. All reveal what goes on right underneath your nose but you're too busy texting and fretting over your IG profile to notice.

For shame.

And not actually living in a port city is a lame excuse.

I would know about this. Ports. Seediness and the like. I was once a Maritime Courier.

I don't put it on my résumé, out of fear of reprisal.

Maritime Couriers service (you guessed it) Maritime Vessels, which are fluvial or more generally waterborne transport for solid or liquid freight, specifically (in my case) things like grain, coal, rock, petroleum, heroin, truck-sized intermodal containers full of stuff we buy at Costco, and occasionally nuclear weapons.

You undoubtedly see the allure, as most do. But don't go rushing to apply for the next Maritime Courier job you see in the newspaper. They don't let just any geek off the street do it. You have to be unemployed, know how to drive a Dodge Caravan, and have a friend whose uncle owns the business.

There's more. Once you've broken through something I've coined "this glass ceiling," you have to know someone within the organization to "vouch" for you, which is a huge deal.

If you pass the vouch, you promptly meet the boss at the bar at 10:00 a.m. and make him a really good Manhattan.

Really good.

If he likes it, your next step is to kill someone and dump the body. If you get away with it, you're in. The whole process takes about a year, at the end of which they give you a hat!

They also give you a phone. Which is unfortunate as you're on call 24 hours a day. The Maritime Courier industry never sleeps. It's like working for Amazon.

I remember my first "job." My friend and I had to go to Bank of America to receive the ship's (don't ever call it a boat, you get hazed if you call it a boat) payroll, which turned out to be about $80,000 in cash. It came in bricks!

Since the boat, er, ship, wasn't coming in until midnight, and it was about 1:00 p.m., my friend and I promptly went to a bar to play pool. The nice thing about pool tables is they have convenient empty spaces underneath for storing backpacks filled with bricks of money while you get another schooner and more quarters. We weren't worried about security, as the bar was packed with its regular retinue of trustworthy, albeit slightly stuporous, day-drinking professionals.

After a harrowing drive we arrived at [undisclosed port city in Washington State] and happily stumbled our way toward the berth (technical term — means "boat parking spot") of the *M.T. Richa*. I know, right? That was its actual name. Merchant vessels frequently come with hilarious monikers like *P&O Nedloyd Senator* or *Marchen Maersk*. However, you should never point out the ridiculousness of this to the captain.

Unfortunately, upon our arrival the berth distinctly lacked this outsized vessel, and in its stead we found a much smaller, much wobblier-seeming metal raft the harbor pilot described as a "skiff," which sounded way less seaworthy than the expected "1,000-Foot Oil Tanker."

Furthermore, the skiff was filled to the brim with foreign language—speaking sailors who seemed all too eager to welcome aboard two land-lubbing losers, er, Maritime Couriers, who nervously tightened the straps of their backpacks, which undoubtedly weren't filled with letters from home, books, or anything short of cash money payroll.

Lest I sound xenophobic, let me assure you that whatever romance language these crew members spoke had no bearing on our sudden realization that perhaps standing on a wobbly boat in the middle of the night in the wind and the rain with a slight hangover and currency that exceeded our combined net worths, all for $15.00/hour (albeit a windfall at the time), was not the best career or general well-being move.

Inevitably the skiff launched across the oily black waters of the harbor, heading for the shadow of a ship one could barely make out through fought-back tears of cowardice. And blowing rain.

Typically when a ship is set to receive crew it magically deploys a gangway, or metal stairway set at 45 degrees to the ship's profile for ease of access. The gangway even has little handrails. Having survived the anticipated gang*plank* (important delineation there) walk (sans money-laden backpacks) during our journey across the harbor, imagine our disappointment as our fellow travelers began to leap onto a dubiously constructed rope ladder dangling off the port side of the *M.T. Nightmare* and deftly scramble their way up the 30 or so feet to the working deck.

I recall asking the skiff's pilot if anyone ever fell in. He said, "Yes. Do you want a life jacket?" I said yes, donned the jacket, and jumped.

I don't remember what my friend did. I know he's not dead.

I do remember pulling myself up to what seemed like the bow of the ship and looking across a thousand feet of pipes and other gadgetry towards the looming-tower part of the tanker — you know, the part with the windows and the bridge and the smokestack where people do the driving.

Maybe it's not called a smokestack anymore.

Assuming my friend was dead, I meandered across the slick deck fighting back sobs and wondering why I went to college. For how long this transpired, I know not, but like a blind pig stumbling upon a truffle, I eventually came across a metal hatchway, behind which lay the most beautiful flight of normal stairs I've ever seen, at the top of which sat a beautiful oak door inlaid with brass work, a portal so stunning I will not see the likes of it again until I knock on St. Peter's gate, offering a false name and otherwise explanatory half-truths.

The captain obviously did not have cowards in his employ, for he looked at my tear-and-snot-covered visage with a mix of confusion and disgust. He then proceeded to hastily count my share of the payroll and, sensing he had a truly overmatched rookie on his hands, tortured me with harrowing tales of merchant marine lore, complete with introductory titles such as these:

Last Week's Gunfight Between Weapons Dealers at [undisclosed port in Washington State]

The Reason Most Couriers Drive Armored Cars Instead of Dodge Caravans

What Happened When Last Month's Drug Shipment Got Interrupted at [undisclosed port in Washington State]

Why You Should at Least Have a "Snake or Something" When Delivering Merchant Vessel Payroll

How Bribes with Port Authorities and Shipping Agents Work at [undisclosed port in Washington State]

Tax Problems Port Authorities and Shipping Agents Face

Security Guards at the Pier: Your Biggest Threat

You May Not Even Make It Home

Luckily my non-dead friend, similarly soaked, snot-covered, and whimpering, interrupted this kind introduction of exactly what I had gotten myself into by pounding on the oak door and screaming "Let me in!" as if being pursued by a pack of velociraptors from *Jurassic Park*. Which prevented my nervous breakdown.

Jurassic Park, not coincidentally, takes place in a port city of sorts.

I lasted a few more months on the job. My friend made it a year. It turns out the life expectancy of a Maritime Courier is similar to that of a mafioso, so after his year my friend actually qualified for his pension.

Ports, piers, pilings, waves — they're all tainted for me now. But I'm glad it happened. It's worth it. Because the next time you glance out the window of your downtown condo at that glimmering water view, maybe you'll look for a tiny shivering figure on the bow of a skiff racing out to sea, bright blonde hair pushed into a lion's mane by the nor'east wind, bottle of whiskey in one hand, bag of money in the other, and you'll know what it's all for; you'll see what you've been missing.

DRYERS

I abhor pictures in the middle of formal web articles.

Unless they're of me, which they never are.

I also get freaked out by backlinks. Whenever I see a backlink in these purported "articles," I make this old man grumpy noise-growl to signal my distaste.

Backlinks stop in my tracks because they seem to have ulterior motives. Like that time in Spain when I was not drunkenly but rather quite innocently walking around a piazza or plaza or whatever they call the Open Area Where Beautiful Spanish People Congregate At Night, and this stranger invited me to play soccer, er, *fútbol* but it turns out he wasn't really inviting me to play soccer, er, *fútbol*; he was distracting me so he could pinch my wallet. Which he did, quite successfully, with relative ease. So that's my problem. Backlinks make me feel like I'm about to get mugged.

I still had fun in Spain.

Obviously I'm in the minority here as I've literally never heard anyone else complain about the ominous presence of pictures or backlinks in web articles. Perhaps, speaking to the backlinks, it's because these particular digital denizens have all the time in the world to click that awkwardly underlined, circa-'90s-Internet-blue-glowing ominous hyperlink and traverse down a wormhole into a completely different realm of supposedly related articles that improve their lives and generally support their journeys toward self-improvement.

I don't have that kind of time.

And the picture in a web article thing? That's just plain lazy. A way to avoid adjectives or setting a scene, kind of like the habit of creating fake descriptors out of hyphenated words because you can't be bothered to think and you rationalize it as funny to absolve the guilt you feel from using such a hack move when technically you have a Bachelor of Arts, English Literature, thank you very much, one of the hardest degrees to obtain at any accredited or unaccredited physical or online college/university in Southwest New Mexico.

But I almost inserted a picture of my dryer into this article.

Do other people in the world use dryers? When I lived in Italy (okay fine, I was on a student exchange program; I wanted to say "lived" to impress you), the first thing I did was find the nearest McDonald's and complain about the distinct absence of dryers.

This resulted in a Beautiful Italian showing me how to hang clothes on a wire, smoke cigarettes, drink red wine, talk about art and Communism, and take a nap. Waking up late in the afternoon (making sure I still had my wallet), I ventured to the wire to find a mysterious force had somehow vaporized the inherent moisture from my garments.

Fascinating.

The proliferation of United States Dryers domestically rather than internationally implies that this kind of European clothesline witchcraft is only available to countries that aren't True Democracies.

I'm fine with this.

Furthermore, if other people in the world used dryers, they'd undoubtedly prefer United States Dryers and we'd have a robust, flashy Dryer Manufacture-and-Export Industry that would significantly bolster our GDP, and we'd see the

PATRICK MCNERTHNEY

main players of this industry frequently grace the covers of *Forbes*, *Inc.* and *International Trade Administration Monthly*.

My dryer, which I will not show here, has some mysterious digital displays and indicator lights installed on its face. Along with some highly suspect marketing copy. The displays, dials, etc. stand out because this dryer is not like the fancy $50,000 chrome-plated, Bluetooth- and TikTok-enabled 2020 Death Robot Dryer that ominously glows in 72 different flavors of neon *you* likely have and can't stop talking about and keep showing your friends every time you have them over for sous vide whatever but secretly they're sick of hearing you talk about how great your dryer and kids are.

No, my dryer is Classic, circa the most coveted year of dryer manufactory, 1997.

So when I see something from 1997 with a bunch of digital displays and indicator lights on it, I'm skeptical because I know for a fact that these things did not exist on any other products of any kind during that time.

Particularly suspect is the "Moisture Monitor" indicator light. It glows red and is vertically oval in shape, with "Moisture Monitor" written as the headline, and "more" above "less" written as the indicator/left-side copy. When I turn on the dryer, the light glows in such a way that it hits both the "more" and "less" copy indicators simultaneously, which at first

102

makes sense as it implies the demon that lives inside recognizes I've put wet clothes in there…but after the device nearly completes its five-hour, 10,000-watt drying cycle, the light *still* glows equally around "more" and "less."

It's a fake, a dummy light. Between episodes of *The X-Files*, some marketing guy told the product engineer to put a "Moisture Monitor" light on this thing so they could charge an extra…hmmm…

…   *retailvalueofcirca1997dryerintodaysdollar-splusinflation* … $10,000!

The same logic likely applies to the aforementioned highly suspect evil marketing copy, which advertises:

"Oversize Capacity Plus,"

"Quiet Plus," and

"Heavy-Duty Intellidry Control."

Come on. "Intellidry"? That's not even a word! At best that's like me calling myself a Creative Director or Vice President of Marketing on my LinkedIn. I don't even know what a Creative Director *does*, let alone remotely fathom the inherent complexities any genius worthy of earning the title "Vice President" in any industry for however brief a period must navigate to deservedly bathe in the admiration of their peers and constantly receive quarterly bonuses immediately after laying off junior staff because sorry we just didn't hit our arbitrary projections but I *definitely* need my bonus.

Ahem. There's a lesson here, storied, enraptured, brilliant, and extremely attractive reader. Look at how the advertising-industrial complex deviously created your need for several dryers in your home, likely one on each floor. Look at those digital displays and pulsating lights, look at the influential *copy,* for goodness' sake. It's no accident. What isn't faked simply to increase your out-of-pocket expense is there to *tell you what to do, influence your decisions, and ultimately trick you into buying more dryers.*

After all, we've determined there's not a dryer to be found in the rest of the world. They've got to sell them somewhere.

Wait. Is there an entire industry dedicated to printing copy on appliances? Ovens, washer/dryers, refrigerators? How does that work? Is it a gigantic typewriter at the end of the production line? Does anyone ever mess with it, like sneak a profanity next to your "Broil" button? I sure would.

We should look into this. Sounds pretty lucrative.

YOU LIKELY NEED PHYSICAL THERAPY

WINTER 2020

My wife is a physical therapist, which means she actually helps people for a living rather than exploiting their weaknesses for financial gain. That's why I married her — she's literally my ticket into heaven.

Which reminds me, I've got a great ground-floor opportunity for you we should discuss by tomorrow afternoon. It's filling up fast. Plus there's free shipping.

I turned 40 (a while back) and as my friend predicted random things started breaking. My sleep. My attention span (I'm no doom scroller but I am a "closest available deep-fried food at midnight" scroller). My shoulder.

I woke up one day and yes, my massive, sculpted, perfectly coiffed, shaven, and tanned right shoulder just started hurting. Like most intelligent men, I waited about six weeks for it to magically go away. Somehow it didn't.

Grudgingly, I went to my primary care doctor and she referred me to this other doctor, of the muscle and spine variety. I think the word "Performance" was somehow incorporated into the marquee at his clinic, right before the word "Medicine," which made me hope anyone who saw me walking in would assume I was a professional triathlete or at least a cross-fit enthusiast, although if I participated in either of those sports right now I'd undoubtedly vomit during warm-ups. Or possibly while putting on my gear. Including a jock strap. I always wear jock straps when I work out.

This doctor did some kind of bait-and-switch maneuver where he had me look over "there," then push against his arm with my forearm or something, and yes he determined I had something wrong with my rotator cuff (which I thought was a myth muscle) and would I like drugs or physical therapy? He didn't even offer me a lollipop. I chose physical therapy.

Now perhaps you're thinking, "Oh cool, your wife is a physical therapist, she can just do it," and I'm here to tell you to wake up and think before you talk. And maybe don't talk out loud to yourself. Having your spouse provide professional services in any capacity is the equivalent of dumping live piranhas and Ginsu knives on your marriage. Plus I whine a lot.

It just so happens that during this time my special lady was taking a class based on the teachings of the Postural Restoration Institute (PRI) in Lincoln, Nebraska. She advised I consult a physical therapist here in town with a PRI certification.

I did. His name was Jeremiah. He looked at my shoulder (admiringly, I will say) and said it hurts because of weakness in my lower left ab wall and furthermore there's nothing wrong with my rotator cuff and please stop taking all the free pens. I insisted that just a week ago my lower left ab wall looked like Brad Pitt's in *Fight Club* and felt even stronger, I'm not sure what happened and why it now looks like a piece of an obese halibut, but sure, I believe you, and you shouldn't leave the pens out if you don't want people to take them. All.

Then he told me to lie on my back, put my feet against a wall, and blow into a balloon. Assuming this was some weird Internet thing likely broadcast to perverts around the world I kind of fake-practiced in the clinic. Then I went home.

For the first time in my life I felt guilty about my skepticism, plus my various health insurance scams (never convicted) put any active claim under a microscope, so I figured I'd give it a try just to finish out the claim. I did this balloon business for five weeks and haven't had a shoulder problem since.

Something happened with my ankle a few months later. I went back, Jeremiah taught me some more insane exercises, one of which involves walking backwards up and down stairs and breathing a certain way, and I was doing it recently in the dark at about 5:45 a.m. and this citizen walked by and oddly enough commented that he liked our blow-up Santa and reindeer decorations rather than on the fact that I'm apparently an insane person obsessively backwards walking and breathing loudly, but I'm glad the decorations brightened his gloomy morning. Oh, and my ankle basically doesn't hurt anymore.

My wife continued her education in this modern-day witchcraft. Lots of hard work. Courses. Tests. Visits to Lincoln, Nebraska, for more tests. Years went by. Decades. I applauded her for bettering herself and trying to help humankind, but I mean where's my homemade mac 'n' cheese, you know? I have to COOK?

Fine.

We even took our son to the Postural Restoration Institute. The inventor guy (I too plan on inventing an institute of some kind one day), who goes by the name Ron Hruska, basically went, "Oh, he needs prism glasses" after about 30 seconds of evaluation, and boom my kid started walking around without a limp, with his head up. See? Witchcraft. My son's too young for placebo so don't go all placebo on me. Although he was given an inordinate amount of sugar pills.

In case you're wondering (you'd better be, this is good for you), there's more to PRI than I'm letting on. It involves breath and breathing, diaphragm usage to balance natural asymmetries in the body, our contact with the ground — a whole host of things I'm not qualified to discuss and am certainly too lazy to research, I mean are you going to pay me for this? Plus I enjoy condensing two decades' worth of positive medical and health explorations, a man's life's work that will benefit humankind, not to mention the hard work of all the super Midwest-nice therapists and staff there, into some pithy commentary.

Also, in case you're wondering, Lincoln, Nebraska, has really good queso. And beef products. I mean seriously good. The queso is white and the edges get kind of thick and chewy and it's liquid cheese I think and the beef basically lives right there in people's backyards. I'd gladly sacrifice my Pacific Northwest salmon and subsequent heart health for an early death at the hands of Lincoln queso and cow. Cows.

Just this month my wife went to Lincoln to take The Ultimate PRI Test, the PRC (Postural Restoration Certified™). She passed, mostly because of my unyielding faith and perhaps the fact that she studied for the better part of oh let's call it a year, with the last six months studying virtually with a peer from Ohio who somehow lives in Vermont. Go figure. I guess if you work hard and stay focused and have a passion…blah blah blah, you've heard it all before.

So, the real message here is I now have a pretty cool T-shirt my wife brought back from her trip, which makes up for my lack of mac 'n' cheese, and this PRI business isn't really witchcraft, it's real, despite the fact that this guy and the Institute don't exactly get mad props from the American Physical Therapy Association.

But that's what happens when you go first and lead, you know? Not everybody gets it right away. And you'll have some haters. But haters are just confused fans. They're into your stuff, they just haven't wrapped their heads around it yet.

WHERE'S THE SHOWMANSHIP?

For some reason I've never been invited to give a speech, virtually or otherwise. Especially not a speech at tech conferences like the Consumer Electronics Show (CES) or AWS re:Invent. Nor have I been invited to orate at healthcare summits like IMSH or the ever-popular AAOS/AANA/AOSSM.

This is likely because it's widely known within both industries that I speak my mind and would thus have the event organizers rename all of their conferences in such a way that these storied events sound like they might actually be fun.

This propensity for directness and clarity has nothing to do with the incident at the 2019 Startup Grind Global Conference, which some misinformation propagators claim was a result of my preference for starting my day with Bellinis, followed by standard Breakfast Proseccos.

What can I say? It was in Redwood City.

But I really thought, what with everything being virtual in 2021, the keynote speaker invites would start pouring in because now the liability is so much lower (they could just turn off my feed or whatever once I went rogue). Plus I'm so incredibly, deliciously affordable. And I'm more than qualified as I (a) use computers and (b) worked in emergency medicine over 15 years ago, so certainly my speaking in a thought-leadership role for both of these industries is just a such a great fit.

Besides, the audience wouldn't be disappointed in my appearance, in the sense that I wouldn't use a well-curated headshot in my official Speaker Bio. I'd just look all dumpy as usual, which would obviously match my onstage persona, so the audience would find this quite refreshing, which in turn would increase demand as word would quickly spread throughout the conference that this guy is on point, yet lighthearted and accessible. And professional. Maybe we should invite him out for a cocktail afterwards?

Perhaps the current problem is organizers around the globe having discovered, despite my expertise and oozing charm, that I'm now excited by clothing that's reversible, and solitude in general, implying I'm an out-of-touch curmudgeon. Or possibly a recluse. But it's not true, as evidenced by the plethora of avant-garde ideas I have for delivering great speeches at technology and/or healthcare summits. It's really quite simple as the topics within these industries are interchangeable. Like reversible clothing.

So here's my pitch to you, thousands upon thousands of slick event organizers reading this. I'd start the speech with my standard Incredible Entrance. This involves walking in with a diamond stud—collared Weimaraner on a leash while eating a hot dog as my assistants set off legitimate, flame-throwing, and frankly quite dangerous pyrotechnics. You've got to get people's attention — especially people who think they're smart, of which 95% of these conferences are comprised.

Next I'd put on not one but two, two of those headsets with the bulbous and quite frankly phallic, plum-sized microphones at the end. That way I'd look twice as important as anyone the audience has seen in  a TED Talk or (vastly inferior) TEDx Talk. Plus I'd look twice as phallic.

As I begin my rapture-inducing presentation, I'd make a huge point of not holding up one hand in front of my sternum (I told you I have a medical background) with thumb, forefinger, and to a lesser degree middle and ring fingers sort of pinched together, as if forming a cusp around an idea. Audiences find that gesture really annoying, and statistics show that it makes them ignore the presenter and start talking to their neighbor. I demand nothing short of absolute, rapt attention when I speak; thus, if I find someone talking to their neighbor during my presentation I will completely and utterly freak out on them, like wedge my way down the middle of the row and scream at them. That will teach the rest of the audience to pay attention and frankly get the most out of my speech. If it's a digital conference, I promise you I have ways of finding you, chatterbox, so help me God.

Whew, sorry about that. I got really worked up there for a second.

Rather than that annoying (and rage-inducing) Tony Robbins "cusp around an idea" hand gesture, I choose to hold my arms out wide during a speech, like super wide, so it's kind of straining my incredible pectorals. It's as if I'm offering the world's biggest hug the entire time — at first it's rather disconcerting based on the heroic volume of armpit sweat I produce at any given moment (my body is highly efficient at cooling itself); however, it eventually becomes endearing.

But this is all window dressing. Albeit really good window dressing. My actual talk is inspired by the United States Marine Corps Basic Training philosophy of "tear them down, then build them back up." Minus the build them back up part. I do this by picking apart the industry I'm speaking to and broadcasting its inherent imperfections and contradictions. It's super easy. Like for tech companies I'd just point out how they have psychological engineering departments specifically designed to make their product incredibly addictive, and thus how the user (i.e., you or I) is the product, and the supposed product is the master, which is really creepy and obviously points to *Terminator 2: Judgment Day*, or anything written by George Orwell.

Or I could bring up Amazon, that's always low-hanging fruit. I'd point out how that company is not really the best option for the consumer, they're just the entrenched option thanks to their vicious (and thus highly applaudable) business practices, including the orchestration of the Prime program to generate unbudgeted, reckless spending not unlike the point-of-sale merchandise rack at a grocery store checkout line. Or the fact that the Last Mile personnel are essentially indentured servants spewing inordinate amounts of carbon dioxide into the air as they deliver my fifth spontaneously ordered "very important item" of the day to my doorstep.

See? People will love this. Tear them down, then let them figure out how to build themselves back up somehow.

For the healthcare summit I don't even have to dive that deep into my material to tear things apart. All you have to do is say "healthcare," "universal healthcare," "premiums," or "medical sales representative" and people get really upset. Then you can just sit back and watch the chaos with your arms spread really wide, which is great because in this case people may really need a hug and maybe they'll take you up on it and you could actually help them feel better. If you're into that kind of thing.

Since I intend this document to serve only as a primer on my techniques, abilities, and expertise in presentation-giving, I'd better stop here. Plus I don't want to give up the whole enchilada. It's bad for business if this format is copied to the degree that I have to come up with new material.

So spread the word. I currently have 167 open "Keynote Speaker" slots on my calendar. And don't think I can't adapt these techniques to your specific industry. Remember, it's not about the knowledge, it's about the show.

GOOD CHEER IS
UNDERVALUED

WINTER 2020

I f I were a rich tycoon, I'd definitely have a National Football Team. Ah, an NFL team. NFL football team. I'd own it. One. Maybe eventually two.

I'd call my first team the Porcelain Mice. Maybe I'll put it in Portland. The Portland Porcelain Mice. But not Portland, Oregon, that place is too trendy plus it basically burned down during The Protests. At least, I think those were protests, or supposed to be protests. It really looked like two hundred days of street brawls. Who do you think is running that whole show anyway? I mean, on both sides of the ball. So to speak. Sorry. But that was a disaster in every way possible, just like my fake passport business in college.

So maybe the Portland, Maine, Porcelain Mice. I hear that place is up and coming. Plus I think it's still around, and I've never had a lobster roll.

It would be really fun recruiting NFL-caliber players to the Porcelain Mice, which the media and Joe Buck (who I find enthusiastic but kind of irritating but I guess that's what folks say about me so I'd better just relax) would affectionately refer to simply as "the Mice."

As in during the NFL draft, the massively ripped guy I'm selecting would excitedly call his mom and say, "The Mice drafted me in the second round — I'm a Mice, I'm a Mice!" Well, wait: "Mouse, I'm a Mouse!" NFL team names can be singular; I looked it up.

The Portland, Maine, Porcelain Mice will have very progressive cheerleaders. That would be my Big Thing. They'll be gay, straight, LGBTQ, men, women, they, them…and eventually representative of every race on the planet — I'm not sure how many races there are, probably a lot, so it'll take a minute to rotate them all in.

Speaking of which, creating all this diversity is going blow the doors off the Cheerleading Industry; I'll likely soon be known as the Father of 21st-Century Cheer. But it will also create some spacing and layout issues. To solve for this I'll happily sacrifice some of the front-row seating in the Mouse Dome (we'll definitely have a dome, the largest ever built) to incorporate my 800-person, completely globally representative cheer squad. Nobody likes those 50-yard-line, front-row fans anyway. In my experience (which is sadly very limited), the more expensive the seat, the more blotto-wasted-crazy the fans get, because rich people are the only ones who can afford the ticket for said seat, 12 beers, and a pretzel (retail value: $4,234).

(I recently learned that all NFL owners profit-share in the alcohol sales at games, as well as any legal fees received by DUI attorneys within 72 miles of the stadium and any bail bond activity within the local metropolitan area. I for one don't have to worry about someone like Jerry Jones profiting from my interaction with law enforcement since I take an Uber to games, but I'm certainly uncomfortable giving him $1.00 every time I buy a beer during the event. That's like giving him $22.00 every Sunday. But it's mostly because in terms of NFL owner caricatures, I mean have you seen Jerry Jones? Talk about looking untrustworthy and over-cologned. Which, when I think about it, is exactly how I'd be if I owned a team, so never mind.)

Ahem. Let's call the cheerleading squad the…ah…well…"the Mice-ettes" is so diminishing…how about we call them "the Fuzzies"? My son has a snake, which means my wife and I have a snake, and in the course of snake parenthood we've learned there are different levels of mice to purchase to feed the slathering monster. In order from small to large: "fuzzies" (which are the cutest), "hoppers," "small adult," "regular adult," and "disgustingly bulbous large." The disgustingly bulbous large ones are heavily regulated by the government because if they ever get out they can actually eat your refrigerator.

Plus, based on the amount of body hair our Globally Progressive Cheer Squad will display, "the Fuzzies" seems appropriate. I wonder if we'll sell a lot of calendars?

But back to the revenue stream, er, the team. The Porcelain Mice. I'd flip the script on the whole ownership model. Sure, I'd hire a General Manager and Head Coach and everything, but I'd basically look over their shoulder the whole time so they know I have their back. Same goes with the players. I may be a horrible athlete and in such bad physical condition that one hit, even at 25% strength, would certainly land me in the emergency room…and I may have never actually played football out of a morbid fear of someone's thigh sweat dripping through my visor, but I'd still involve myself in their training, offering lots of tips 'n' tricks from my schoolyard days, especially during crucial moments of the game. I think they'd respect me for that.

I'd also involve myself in the uniform design, which is secretly why I'm getting involved with the NFL in the first place. I'd encourage everything, top to bottom, to be in a literal rainbow of colors, to symbolize our operational, coaching, and frankly game management philosophy of just plain not moving too fast, stopping and enjoying the moment, looking for life's rainbows. Same deal, I'd expect tons of respect for that — and lots of interviews.

Finally, I would literally profit share with all the players and the Fuzzies (cheerleaders are vastly underpaid). I read a football book about the Chicago Bears once (I forgot the title and I'm too lazy to look it up for you), and I remember the author stated, "…make no mistake, the players make millions because the owners make billions." Maybe it wasn't that book — maybe I just read it online. But since I believe it to be true it's true, and I only need one simple billion. Multiple billions makes you just plain greedy and vain, and I want no part in that. Plus the players deserve it, given their direct exposure to extreme violence and thigh sweat.

So that's the Porcelain Mice, featuring the Fuzzies.

Team number two needs some work. I'm open to your suggestions, but before you submit them you have to sign a form that states you surrender all the rights to your ideas (all ideas in general, not just the NFL stuff). To me.

TECHNICALLY HITCHCOCK
COVERED THIS

The house across the street from us, well kind of diagonally across the street and a few houses down so I think that's called kitty-corner+10, is grey with white trim and 4,000 feet tall. Four thousand feet.

It used to be dumpy and brown, and a recluse-type person lived there. The house right next door to it was red at the time and had a carport. Carports are an anomaly in Seattle and generally seem to be a throwback to 1977. I half expect them to be carpeted.

Eventually we figured out that some ne'er-do-wells lived in the carport house and they sold drugs.

Seattle's real estate is expensive. So are the groceries. Maybe that's why the carport people sold drugs. We bought our house in 2000-can't-remember, and it wasn't the crappiest house on the block but it wasn't the nicest and I wouldn't call it affordable so certainly I sort of reluctantly accepted the recluse and the carport drug dealers, with more sympathy falling toward the recluse. Whom I never actually saw, which isn't surprising.

Eventually the drug dealers moved away, and with them went the smell of barbecue. NOT grilling. Grilling is when you cook beef on a grill and blue smoke comes out and things splatter and smell delicious with cheese. Barbecue is when you cook meat at extremely low temperatures for pretty much all day in a "smoker," which has a place for you to throw in wood chips so they ignite, infusing your delicious meats with smoke from say, oh, pecan wood is my favorite.

Don't feel bad for being so ignorant that you frequently say "barbecue" when you mean "grill." I was once an ignoramus too, until my Kansan father-in-law smacked me when it became apparent my marriage to his daughter was perfectly legal and binding yet I didn't know the difference between barbecuing and grilling.

Okay, he didn't actually smack me, but I know he wanted to.

Oh, crack smells like barbecue when you smoke it.

So no drug dealers equals no crack smokers equals no barbecue smell. Except when you're grilling, er, smoking meat. As long as you're not also smoking crack. But you wouldn't do that because you'd end up getting all tweaked out and rushing the barbecuing process, which is a bad idea.

The 4,000-Foot-Tall House with the Recluse housed a type of recluse who decided one day to answer his front door with a very rifle-looking BB gun. It was either in response to the postal worker or social worker knocking on his door, I can't remember which.

This created a situation.

One that we didn't know was transpiring while we were having dinner at home with my brother and sister-in-law.

Why does "eating" dinner sound so crude but "having" dinner apropos? If someone used "apropos" in a real out-loud sentence, I'd probably punch them. Forget I even used that word. To be honest, I had to look up what exactly it meant. And worse, I used Google to do so (sob).

As we stood on our porch saying our farewells post-consumption that fateful summer night, I noticed an untoward amount of police people, complete with *Hill Street Blues*—style pointy cop hats, sort of swarming all over our intersection. As my in-laws reached their white

Volkswagen Jetta, they suggested we retreat inside, as indicated by their frantic hand gesticulations that seemed to mimic the universally accepted "back up," "retreat," or "run from tiger" signal. You know, kind of a cupped-hand, fingers splayed, snapping at the wrist, high-paced wave. But more stressed out.

After hurriedly shoving my wife aside and diving into our foyer for cover (same thing, if someone said "foyer" out loud, I'd hit them), I grudgingly decided the Internet was required to determine our best next steps as I was very concerned for her safety.

I visited the mildly pornographic neighborhood site myballard.com. After navigating past a bunch of truly weird stuff, I found the police blotter/911 feed, which indicated SWAT had just arrived to cordon off the streets in front of my house and trample through people's rosebushes. And possibly shoot the recluse.

In 2020 Seattle passed a big defund-the-police initiative, so the police are being defunded, with the defunds supposedly being reappropriated to mental health and other unarmed interventionalists to better serve the community. Maybe that would have been good to have this night. Or bad, I can't say. I'm all for providing more resources to the community, particularly nonviolent resources. But defunding the police seems like a bad way to grow a program of unarmed interventionalists.

Like most normal people facing mortal danger, my wife and I decided to go to bed. I tried to get her to sleep on the high-likelihood-of-crossfire side of the mattress, but she wouldn't bite. She fell blissfully asleep on the safe side. I just kind of lay there listening to various official police yellings, including several through a megaphone, as the red-and-blue flashing lights from the cop cars bounced off my ceiling and I wondered if my property tax would go up or down as a result of these happenings.

Eventually some flash-bang grenades went off someplace. I could tell by the very bright flashes that cascaded through my window, and the loud, explosive bang-type noises that accompanied them.

Then I heard a few pops. And went to sleep.

I was young then, young and vibrant and full of life, no real anxieties, which I think is why I went to sleep. Now I sleep with an eye mask à la Dick Van Dyke because our front porch light is too bright but I don't want to turn it off out of fear some teenagers will show up and ransack my living room. I also frequently wonder whether our room is too hot and thus how much money we could save by leaving the thermostat at 67 degrees. And I often need to take Tums if I have a rich meal. So now I doubt I could sleep through a neighborhood gunfight. Youth is truly wasted on the young, as it were.

The next morning as I walked around the neighborhood looking for crack cocaine, I noticed the property of interest hadn't been burned down and the cops were gone, yet they decided to leave a bullet-sized hole in what appeared to be the upper bedroom window of this poor man's home.

The neighbor across the street (from both the super tall, newly bullet-holed house and my house…it's hard to explain…I guess kitty corner+5) later told me they arrived home from a nice meal that night (this neighbor scores films for a living; his first film was *Die Hard 3*, which is an interesting first film to score but he's not complaining, given that his house is 5,000 square feet with a roof deck) only to find SWAT snipers stationed in their really nice, kind of romantic to my understanding master bedroom. Which the cops who allowed them to re-enter their house in the first place sort of forgot to mention.

Which created a uniquely awkward moment where upon entering their bedroom they had to kind of tiptoe-backpedal downstairs to their expansive living room (complete with a $30,000 Italian cello on a pedestal under a museum-like spotlight — I guess he's a classically trained cellist, which explains his action movie-scoring acumen, sort of) until the shooting stopped.

Well, started. Then stopped.

This rich neighbor said the SWAT guys took a shot at the recluse but missed, then decided to use nonlethal ouchie heavy beanbag rounds, which encouraged this poor fellow to surrender. Well, that and the real bullet whizzing by his head.

The 4,000-Foot-Tall House sat vacant for many years after this incident, complete with bullet-hole-in-bedroom-window. Then some enterprising bottom-feeder came and remodeled it into the beautiful grey-stucco-with-white-trim urban mansion that it is. I wonder if this house flipper had to disclose the whole gunplay thing to the buyer. Is there a line item for that kind of thing on all those forms you sign when you buy a house? Is understanding the forms the only thing that makes a Realtor® a Realtor®? Is it that simple, and we're all easily capable of being Realtors® but don't know it, just like my American Government teacher said we could all do just as good a job as any politician if we were Representatives or Senators or Presidents or the Wealthy Agents of Multinational Corporations who pay their salaries?

There was a point when a sinkhole erupted right in front of this cursed property during the "flip." It didn't swallow anything or anyone, and I got some good mileage out of the backhoe loaders and excavators that subsequently lived there for several months (my son was three at the time, and heavy construction equipment is like Turkish delight to little kids). But I couldn't help but think the cosmos was suggesting maybe this place should be left alone for a while or turned into a park or something. And maybe the new owner shouldn't park his Tesla there. And maybe we don't know as much about what's going on around us as we think.

BEARS, BLOOD, AND GOLDEN TEE – NOT NECESSARILY IN THAT ORDER

WINTER 2021

This guy's blood squirted pretty much on me at the start of our honeymoon. I was a brand-new tech in an ER, and I wanted this healthcare/emergency services gig to bolster my resume as I attempted to enter the fire service despite a healthy fear of heights, fire, and driving oversized vehicles. Wanted it so bad that when a scheduling error resulted in my required presence during what should have been my first glorious night of matrimony, I found myself clamping my hand down on the arm of a very hairy man with bad veins.

My wife was safe and sound in the Salish Lodge & Spa, where we had checked in earlier as part of our first day of Honeymoon Spectacular-ness, possibly snuggled under warm blankets next to a toasty fire, given that it was October. After holding that guy's veins closed, helping restrain a violently delirious meth addict, getting reprimanded for giving a homeless guy a sandwich (long story), changing a colostomy bag, getting offered $500 to swap pee with a guy who rolled his car at 90 miles an hour on I-5 (I didn't take him up on the offer, so I'm assuming he failed his drug/alcohol screen), inserting some catheters, getting yelled at by a cop for almost using an alcohol wipe before a blood draw on a DUI suspect (defense attorney would claim the alcohol wipe influenced the blood test), and almost vomiting while collecting a stool sample (that bodily emission was the only thing that made me queasy), I had just enough time to drive the 30 miles back to my new wife, have a celebratory cocktail, and pass out.

She probably would have preferred I change out of my bloody scrubs, but I was tired.

Not ones for dismay-ment, we awoke at dawn, day two of The Most Fantastic Honeymoon Ever Recorded, ready to get the party started. We had a tight itinerary, with the first stop (well technically the second stop) being a one-night stay at a bed & breakfast located at the universally accepted World's Greatest Winery in Yakima, Washington, which is actually one of the principal drug distribution centers in North America. In fact, the Sinaloa Cartel smuggles heroin and meth in 18-wheelers and cars with hidden compartments from Mexico up I-5, then through Yakima and onward. Which is, well, probably not conducive to the success of Yakima's wine industry or any certification as The World's Greatest anything, but it didn't deter the likes of us.

Our Honeymoon Vehicle of Choice, well really of no choice, was my wife's 2000 Volkswagen Jetta. It turns out the 2000 Volkswagen Jetta was the First New Model Year in a while. Which means it was a new design, and in this case from a new manufacturing location. Namely, Mexico. Now, despite the drug reference, I have nothing against Mexico or its manufacturing industry. However, I now have something against the first time a German product is manufactured in Mexico. My first clue that something was amiss was the fact that the interior driver's side door handle came off in cartoonish fashion when one attempted to close the door. Wires hanging out and everything. Furthermore, given that Washington is a community property state, I realized that perhaps a dowry would have been a nicer addition to my marriage than a German/Mexican import, but my love knows no bounds, as she will attest.

On our way to one of the principal drug distribution centers in North America, the water pump in this Jetta gave out. We'd made it about 18 miles from the Salish Lodge & Spa, where obviously we should have just stayed and ordered massages and room service.

We limped into Scenic North Bend, Washington (home of that café in Twin Peaks, if you're old enough to remember that series which you're probably not which makes me mad. And birthplace of Salvador Dali, who also appeared in the series; you can look it up).

Fortunately, and we were ripe with fortune, we found a lonely, nonviolent-seeming mechanic open on a Saturday. We dutifully awaited his verdict for our repair timeframe in a cozy dive bar that featured Pabst in plastic pitchers and everyone's favorite bar game, Golden Tee. I'm fairly certain I lost every game to my betrothed, thus I refuse to play with her ever again because I'm a sexist and a sore loser.

A few hazy hours later, said verdict came in: Our Mexican car was going to be stuck in Scenic North Bend for several days. My wife's tears (genuine) encouraged this isolated fellow to give us a loaner car. He didn't have loaner cars; it was a Honda Civic he just sort of realized he had in the corner. Which upon reflection makes me realize there was likely no title or insurance or anything legal about it, kind of like when someone pulls up next to you in a van and offers to (for cash) sell you new stereo equipment they somehow just found (this has happened to me about six times in my life; if it hasn't happened to you, there's something wrong with you). We unknowingly accepted the legal risk and sprinted the remaining 114 miles to our winery bed & breakfast/drug distribution hub.

Our room featured lots of drapes and other fabrics adorned with images of stemmed cherries, which is weird and instantly made me think this was a cartel operation because it's not like they're going to interior-design their safe houses with images of needles and opium poppies; no way, they'd use fresh fruit. But we were out of options, and it wasn't like I was going to make my wife sleep in the car (I waited a few years later for her to be pregnant to do that).

Given that we had to depart at 4:00 a.m. the next morning for leg three of our journey and would thus miss the implied breakfast portion of our "bed &," the matron prepared a fancy, honeymoon-worthy dinner for us. Which we missed, as we rolled in about six hours late, roughly 10:30 p.m.

Never to be…dismayed, we slept maybe four hours and awoke for the 157-mile drive to Lake Chelan, Washington, for our date with *The Lady of the Lake*, a mighty interior oceangoing vessel with a departure time of 8:00 a.m. Destination — the Honeymooners' Paradise of the North Cascades: Stehekin, Washington.

As we gathered on the dock, exhausted and starving, we noticed a distinct absence of young, vibrant, extremely attractive honeymooners such as ourselves. In fact, the observable passenger population consisted of about 40 significantly senior citizens, eight bearded deer hunters, and a fortunately sober-seeming captain. But we were almost to paradise, time to press on.

Lake Chelan runs roughly 55 miles long amidst the mountains of north-central Washington. Really pretty. We had plenty of time to take in this natural splendor as *The Lady of the Lake* is not one to rush; it bubbled along at 13 miles an hour (I won't do the knot conversion), for a total cruising time of four hours with no food or drink or I'm pretty sure a bathroom. Of course there was a faster boat called *The Cheetah of the Lake* or something, but we weren't adept at interpreting metaphors at the time. Then there were the floatplanes, but what kind of snob takes a floatplane to commute? A rich smart one, it turns out.

Plus *The Lady of the Lake* makes stops along the way. Two maddening, long stops. The latter of which involved beaching on the shoal at the base of this terrifying mountain where I anticipated a counterattack by jug- and banjo-wielding hillbillies. None appeared, so with all their gear the crazy deer hunters waded ashore, the youngest of which looked terrified as this was obviously his first week-long wilderness deer hunt, which undoubtedly would involve lots of gas, body odor, and other camaraderie from his older, more well-seasoned mates.

Eventually the mighty *Lady* berthed at the dock of our Honeymoon Arc de Triomphe, the Lodge at Stehekin. As our senior citizen companions happily hopped — well, kind of hobbled — onto said dock with the help of the Lodge staff, we kept kind of looking beyond the weathered, dilapidated structure in hopes of catching a glimpse of the 21st- or even 20th-Century Updated Nice Lodge that surely lay in the trees beyond or something. But the glimpse would not be caught. After careful consideration of the likelihood of going insane by taking another four-hour boat ride back to civilization, we succumbed to what by now could only be described as our Honeymoon Fate.

Upon check-in at the Official Reception Desk, we were greeted by a lovely junior college student wrapping up her tour of duty at the Lodge. I can still see her completely terrified expression upon learning we were there on our Official Honeymoon, coupled with her words, "You're here on your honeymoon?" Pause as she furtively glanced at the confused seniors milling about. "I'm sorry."

Stehekin can only be reached by boat or seaplane. There are approximately six miles of paved roads, with another six miles of unpaved Forest Service roads. The few cars in the area hearken to the Castro regime, complete with registration tabs from the '60s and '70s. Hiking and outdoor activities are the main pastimes, but there are more civilized amenities, including an outdoor pool and supposedly amazing bakery, all of which had closed two weeks prior in anticipation of winter and the subsequent heavy snowfall.

One fantastic amenity for non-woodsy, civilized folk turned out to be the lack of television inside the pool-felt-green-carpeted cabins, combined with a plethora of board games. Thus I learned that my wife, who hadn't divorced me yet, was an adept, if not ruthless, Rummikub player. And Trivial Pursuit player. And blackjack player. And Monopoly player.

Luckily breakfast and lunch featured a fabulous buffet in the dining hall, the majority of which consisted of previously frozen and boxed delights from prominent National Foodservice Distributors, including U.S. Foods, Sysco, and to a lesser degree, Costco. I was actually in heaven. My bride, not so much.

During our second night in Stehekin (my mind, in an effort at self-preservation, has wiped itself clean regarding the total length of our stay), a man emerged from the woods on some insane hike from Canada to Mexico or something. A real provider. A real man's man. I made sure my wife didn't see him, for fear of comparison. This same night, the Lodge staff made a lovely announcement regarding our recent vows, to the applause and delight and occasional dirty-old-man catcalls of our fellow, albeit quite older, guests.

Which turned out to be an omen, for at breakfast the next morning a table had been reserved for a true Honeymoon Breakfast of heat lamp—warmed sausage patties and hash brown rectangles. And, as it turns out, 40 handwritten notes from our new friends at Stehekin Lodge, wishing us the best for our future together, including general lovely wishes, sage advice, and several dirty limericks. Luckily they did not include drawings. By now I knew who the prime suspects were.

After realizing we were on the honeymoon equivalent of Gilligan's island, we finally decided to make the best of it and go for a hike. Hitchhiking is legal in this lawless land — apparently having only 12 miles of roads in total makes the area exempt from Washington State's RCW 46.61.260, which prevents one from soliciting rides — likely because there are no revenue generation requirements for local law enforcement, if there even is local law enforcement, which is why if I ever have to make my first hit to join the Mafia I'll do it in Stehekin. Thus we started up the paved road that turned into a dirt road and caught a ride from a Forest Ranger.

Unfortunately, he decided to regale us with stories about the abundance, I daresay bunny-like proliferation, of bears in the area. During this time I noticed my wife became somewhat pale and wide eyed, but I assumed she was experiencing the cascading elation commonplace when spending significant amounts of time with me.

It turns out she's scared of bears. The Ranger dropped us off at a trailhead six miles up the

road, and we began a beautiful, easy ascent
into the (eerily) quiet pine woods of the
region. As soon as the forest enveloped us, my
wife froze and declared it was time to return
home. Which home, I wasn't sure, but I did know
the trail was a horseshoe loop, so either way
we had to walk at least six miles. In the
woods.

Luckily, she came up with an incredibly
practical solution. She picked up two rocks and
every 50 feet began clacking them together and
shouting, "No bears!" Over. And over and over.
I explained that bears really aren't interested
in people, they're interested in garbage cans
and potentially picnic baskets, of which we had
none. Furthermore, any bear within 25 miles was
probably sitting on its haunches having a good
laugh with its bear friends and other fellow
woodland creatures, and possibly a piglet.

All to no avail. The clacking and shouting
continued through the pristine landscape. That
is, until my wife, who is extraordinarily fit
and determined, grew fatigued and asked that I
resume the cacophonic march. Which, as a new
husband and generally considerate person, I
did, although somewhat abashedly, given that I
consider myself a bit of a hunter and light
outdoorsman.

Obviously, we made it through this hike and
encountered nothing short of incredible views
of the lake and the occasional bee, who was not
at all impressed or intimidated by our rock-

clacking security measures. From this point on, the rest of the trip is a blur. At checkout we anted up and took *The Cheetah of the Lake* back to civilization — we'd had enough of our Honeymoon Destiny. We did keep all the notes from the old people though, including the dirty limericks. They're down in the basement somewhere.

Oh! Our car wasn't ready when we arrived back in North Bend, so a few days later I had to go back and pick it up (secretly sneaking into that dive bar for a pint and solo game of Golden Tee, just so I could win).

Technically, 15 years later, I still owe my wife a replacement honeymoon in Italy, something we came up with on the drive home. But I have to be honest, one of the reasons I haven't booked it yet is it can't possibly be as interesting, no matter how old that place is.

FOCUS GROUPS ARE JUST AN EXCUSE TO MAKE OUT

FALL 2020

Technically one could walk around one's neighborhood and turn off people's gas mains.

Then you'd have Total Control. You could be the Mayor of about four square blocks. "He who controls the Spice, controls the universe" and all that.

The Spice in this case is a metaphor for natural gas. It's kind of a stretch if you haven't read *Dune* or witnessed the abomination of a film of the same name made in 1984 and starring that guy from *Twin Peaks*. Kyle what's-his-name.

It's not super easy. Gas mains have a little shut-off valve, kind of oval in shape, cast from a quarter-inch worth of flat steel, with a little hole at the end. You can either grasp the flat of the valve with a wrench and turn it until perpendicular with the pipe, or use a 4-in-1 emergency tool that will fit in the provided hole and similarly rotate the valve closed.

Your main advantage is that 73.45% of homeowners don't even know they have a gas main, according to the Department of Housing and Urban Development. The odds are in your favor. How can you NOT do this?

As Mayor you could then demand daily "fire rent" in exchange for providing people access to their gas for five minutes at about 1/16th the normal flow rate. If there are 44 houses per block, and you lord over four square blocks, and each house pays you $8.99 (according to the American Marketing Association, pricing is most effective when rounded down to the hundredth of a dollar, a.k.a. "penny," which you can now rename "surlap" or whatever crazy word you want because you're the de facto Mayor), this provides you with about $2,657.72 of revenue per day once you subtract the gas bill (somebody has to pay it), enough to buy a top hat suitable to wear at a jaunty angle like the crazed governors who control the barren landscapes of various apocalyptic full-length feature films.

How great would that be?

The biggest risk lies not in getting caught, but rather in your storytelling ability. Explaining why you're on someone's property, especially when it likely involves burying yourself deep in the surrounding foliage, is dangerous business. But as with all good speeches and/or PowerPoint presentations, if you look like you know what you're doing, if you speak with an air of glaring confidence that conveys a penchant for physical altercations and an eager willingness to challenge the listener's entire belief system to the point that they readily question the existence of their soul, it's fairly easy to pull off.

"Oh, my neighbor said Amazon left her package here," spoken as a threat, with a big smile, icy glare, and requisite matter-of-factness, works wonders. In fact, the weirder the explanation, the better, as long as you avoid keywords that rhyme with misdemeanors and/or felonies. "I'm on your property because" or "I'm here because" spoken nervously screams malfeasance and will likely result in the homeowner reaching into their flowered robe for their switchblade, dog, automatic weapon, or (if you're lucky) phone with which to call the authorities.

Oh, you're likely committing a misdemeanor.

But according to the International Association of Defense Counsel (IADC), there's a very fine line between hijinks and misdemeanors, so you should be good. To clarify your intentions and how your future court case will play out, as well as provide an intellectual understanding of how to navigate our legal system, think of it like this: You're not walking around shutting off people's gas mains in an effort to commit domestic terrorism or cause any suffering. You're just looking to do some hijinks, which are victimless crimes judges sometimes confuse with misdemeanors. According to the IADC.

This is all beside the point. The sad truth is the percentage chance of any confrontation as a result of getting caught rummaging around your neighbors' azaleas falls below 3%, according to the Bureau of Labor and Statistics and the National Gardening Association. Which is the same percentage of people that pay attention to your speech/PowerPoint presentation despite how much you fret over it, according to the Federal Communications Commission.

Both are direct results of the human condition known as Not Reacting to Things That Are Boring, according to the American Psychological Association.

People just don't like boring stuff. And they don't like doing work. They like to just sit there, mouth-breathe, and move as little as possible. Apple Inc. is actually working on an iPhone that levitates in front of your face off a magnet you wear on your forehead. The heat from a concentrated stare at a given app operates said app (eyes are very hot, according to the American Optometric Association; they emanate up to 23% of our body heat).

Originally Apple's plan was to have this floating phone operate off puffs of breath aimed at the screen through pursed lips, but focus group testing showed users just ended up making out because everyone's maws just looked so juicy and inviting. Furthermore, at the conclusion of this study, participants somewhat offhandedly reported that puffing sounded like TOO MUCH WORK TO OPERATE A PHONE, according to the American Statistical Association.

Unbelievable. So you've got nothing to worry about. To the average bear, the fact that you're fussing with the gas main garners virtually no interest. Messing with a window? Attention-garnering because it closely resembles a criminal act, and according to the National Association of Realtors®, people's fear of declining home values because of crime is the number one reason they stand up to look outside. But a gas main? Meh. Boring. What's a gas main do anyway?

Herein lies your opportunity for hijinks, public office, and a steady revenue stream. What are you waiting for?

AVIAN SPECIAL FORCES COMMUNITIES

FALL 2020

It's hunting season, and no matter how you feel about that you should know tofu is regularly hunted in the central portion of the United States. The blocks wobble their way down to Mexico from Canada in one of nature's greatest migrations, second only to the flight of the Monarch butterfly. Thus from North Dakota straight down through Texas, riflemen and riflewomen set up their tree blinds and pick off the squishy blocks one by one until their daily bag limit is reached and they can return home to make pho.

Tofu hunters are a weird lot; I prefer to stay away from them and hunt pheasant and duck instead.

Pheasants are directly related to velociraptors, which is why we're allowed to hunt them (the Department of Fish and Wildlife absolutely does not want to see pack-hunting dinosaurs return to our verdant wheat fields and scrublands anytime in the foreseeable future).

Pheasants prefer walking/running on the ground over taking flight, only becoming airborne when a predator flushes them from cover. So basically you need a dog to encourage their flight…if you just walk around, the pheasants keep walking/running away from you, never leaving the ground, kind of chuckling to each other in the process, which makes you look like an idiot.

Finally, you can only shoot the boy pheasants. The girl pheasants are protected, which is obviously discriminatory. So you better be good at telling the boys from the girls. It takes a lot of practice — identifying bird genitalia at 50 yards as they take flight requires years of study and subsequent certification, from apprentice to journeyman to…whatever the last one is. Plumber?

Oh, last thing: To hunt pheasants you need to wear a bunch of neon orange clothing, from hats to vests to pants, so you don't get shot by other hunters. Fun! It's worth it; pheasants taste like exotic chickens. And literally anyone can do it. You just need a birth certificate from somewhere on Earth and a gun.

Ducks are an entirely different matter. Most people don't realize that ducks are the Special

Forces of the bird community, closely related to the Navy SEALS in particular, given their ability to operate on sea, air, and land…and to quack. Most people also don't realize Navy SEALS quack to indicate when a threat is approaching. Just like a perturbed duck.

Ducks have incredibly good eyesight. Before we continue, we should point out there's a huge difference between a wild duck and that big fat bread-eating duck in the park next to your house. The latter has great eyesight too but can't be bothered to even muster a squint because he/she is coddled into obesity and complacence by cute, sourdough-wielding children or that eccentric guy in the overcoat who goes to the park by himself to smoke cigarettes, mutter under his breath, and drink fortified wine. While feeding ducks.

The incredible eyesight of wild ducks requires duck hunters to spend thousands of dollars on truly terrible-looking camouflage pants, jackets, hats, gloves, masks, hip boots, waders, blinds, guns, thermoses, coolers…everything.

It's actually a form of economic warfare wild ducks have learned through evolution. Chipping away at the credit rating and financial stability of their pursuers has led to increased duck birth rates for the past two decades. Fact.

Some hunters have actually tried building their own customized giant duck costume to save some money. It's a head-to-toe, zip-in-the-back-type outfit, including a three-foot bill, the recess of which frames their human face. It works to a degree, but inevitably those cagey wild ducks sense something is awry as they witness their six-foot cousins reaching widely around their beaks with their feathered arms to smoke, drink a beer, or eat a sandwich. Normal ducks don't eat with their wings. Or smoke.

The other burdens duck hunters bear are ungodly hours, dismal weather conditions, and inhospitable terrain. Pheasant hunting is a spa day in comparison, what with the chance to walk around wheat fields in 75-degree sunshine, with Snickers bars in your pocket and a 12:00 sharp lunch date at some small-town diner.

Duck hunters have to get up before dawn, march around a marsh or estuary or soggy field in the dark to find a blind (thing you hide behind), basically stay perfectly still for six-plus hours no matter how freezing or rainy it is (it's that eyesight thing), make sure the tide doesn't trap you there all day (or night) if you're near saltwater…and so on and so forth.

Maybe duck hunters are as weird as tofu hunters after all. All the bizarre clothes, financial and physical hardships…who takes part in that voluntarily?

Regardless, if being mocked by Mother Nature in these ways doesn't appeal to you, or you just don't want to harvest an animal, there's all sorts of other hunting you can do. Truffle. Chantarelle. Spouse. House. But don't kid yourself. Think about the absolute weirdness inherent in these activities before you get all judge-y. I feel safer walking around a field full of shotgun-wielding, camouflaged nerds than getting between two Realtors® at an open house.